CW00487243

Walking the Coastline of Shetland

No. 2

The Island of Unst

Peter Guy

The coastline and inland circular walks
in Unst and the islands of Uyea and Balta.

Published by
The Shetland Times Ltd.,
Lerwick, Shetland.
2002

First published by The Shetland Times Ltd., 2002

ISBN 1 898852 76 6

Text © Peter Guy, 2002

Photographs © Peter Guy except where otherwise acknowledged.

A CIP catalogue record for this book is available from the British Library.

Books in the same series

No. 1 The Island of Yell
No. 3 The Island of Fetlar
No. 4 Northmavine
No. 5 Westside
No. 6 South Mainland

Cover photographs by Bobby Tulloch.

Front:
The dramatic cliffs of Unst;
Britain's most northerly house – the Haa of Skaw;
Edmondston's Chickweed.

Back:
Unst gannets at sunset.

Printed and published by
The Shetland Times Ltd., Prince Alfred Street, Lerwick,
Shetland ZE1 0EP, Scotland.

Dedicated to the memory of Bobby Tulloch, Shetland's outstanding naturalist who introduced me and many others to the coastline of Unst, particularly the cliffs at Hermaness.

Also Magnie Sinclair of Haroldswick who shared his enthusiasm and knowledge about several delightful aspects of life on Unst, not least the celebration of Old Christmas. On Old Christmas Eve particularly his home became a happy place to assemble and it is fitting that there are now plans to make his home into a Camping Böd for the access and enjoyment of all visitors to Unst.

For Georgina Kerensa.

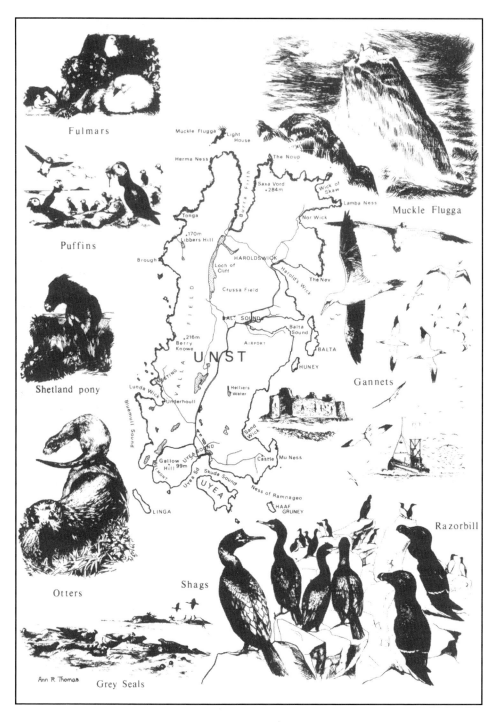

Fulmars

Puffins

Shetland pony

Otters

Grey Seals

Muckle Flugga Light House

Herma Ness

The Noup

Saxa Vord
.284m

Wick of Skaw

Lamba Ness

Tonga

Nor Wick

.170m
Libbers Hill

Brough

HAROLDSWICK

Loch of Cliff

Harold's Wick

The Nev

Crussa Field

BALT SOUND

Balta Sound

.218m
Berry Knowe

AIRPORT

BALTA

UNST

HUNEY

Lunda Wick

VALLA FIELD

Helliers Water

FIELD

Bluemull Sound

Underhoull

Sand Wick

Gallow Hill 99m

UYEA SOUND

Castle Mu Ness

Uyea Sd

Ness of Ramnageo

UYEA

LINGA

HAAF GRUNEY

Muckle Flugga

Gannets

Razorbill

Shags

Ann R Thomas

6

Walking the Coastline of Shetland No. 2

THE ISLAND OF UNST

60 Miles (100 Kilometers)

Unst, the most northerly inhabited island in Great Britain, deserves to be visited by all people who call themselves British. The dramatically beautiful windswept islands of Shetland, particularly the island of Unst, confirm the diversity and splendour of our country and the individual nature of the people who inhabit it. Why stop at Land's End or John O'Groats?

The rewards of making the journey to the farthest north are immense and the enjoyment will be that much greater if Unst can be explored on foot.

Unst is home to about 1000 people, it measures 47 square miles and is the third largest of the Shetland Islands (Mainland is 378 square miles, Yell 83). It is 12 miles (19kms) in length from north to south by 5 miles (8kms) in breadth on average. Unst boasts 60 miles of varied coastline, all of which can be trod by the average walker.

The scenery is excellent. There is not much peat in Unst and the variety of underlying rock gives the surface colouring a bright and varied appearance. The geological map of the island is kaleidoscopic.

When I was serving in the Royal Air Force and subject to frequent postings I went to see the well-known Lincolnshire fortuneteller 'The Blind man of Market Deeping'. I asked him to confirm a rumour that I was due for another move shortly and he replied that, yes, I was. "You are going to an island", he said. I had only recently returned from Penang island in Malaysia so I asked him, "Are the trees on the island pine or palm?" There was a considerable delay before he eventually replied, "I can see no trees at all". The relevance of this remark escaped me until I flew into Baltasound on a Loganair flight on posting to RAF Saxa Vord. I scanned the land beneath me. The old boy was right, there were "no trees at all". (He actually missed "Saxby's Forest" which we will find on Walk 8).

I discovered that fitness enthusiasts at Saxa Vord had created the 'Round Unst Trek' – an annual challenge to walk the entire coastline of Unst over a summer weekend. Years later an intrepid BP colleague of mine at Sullom Voe, technical manager Frank Musgrave, walked the 60 mile 'RUT' in 22 hours sleeping for a while in a 'bivvy bag' on Burrafirth beach.

This book is not written with that sort of target in mind but for walkers who wish to savour the experience with more time available. The first part of the book presents the walk round Unst as a long distance footpath. Some of these coast walks are well suited to "there and back" walks. For linear walks, if a combination of car and cycle is utilised, as I do, then the walks can be enjoyed independently of any transport support.

The second part suggests various loop or circular walks as well as covering visits to Balta and Uyea islands.

Unst is a treasure house of natural and historic features and tramping it will be a memorable and enjoyable experience.

Good walking!

Peter Guy

Lerwick,
Shetland.

Life in Shetland is not quite like city life.

There are no huddled houses, noisy streets and din of smoking factories and workshops. There are open spaces and fresh air, light, sunshine. Out in the country the loudest noises in some places are the din of swarming birds on the cliffs, or the lowing of kye and bleating of sheep.

At times the kye and the birds are silent, the sheep quiet on the hills; but for the echoing cries of a crofter sending his dog after some stray sheep a kirkyard quiet seems to brood over the place.

An extract from a letter:
From *"Letters in Shetland"* Peter Jamieson

GETTING TO UNST

Unst is normally reached through a combination of road and inter-island ferries and as you cross Yell the first view of it will be at the junction with the road to Basta, for it is from this point that the hills of west Unst can be seen, reaching their peaks at Valla Field and dominating the northern skyline.

At Gutcher, just after the crossroads to Cullivoe and North Sandwick, pull off the road to admire the view up the Blue Mull Sound as far as South Geo of Brough, whilst to the east the gaunt ruin of the hall on the island of Uyea can be seen.

Passage to Belmont on Unst will be by car ferry, one of the second generation of Shetland Island Council inter-island ferries. Do not be surprised if you are escorted to the ramp by a small party of domestic geese; the 'Gutcher Geese' have adopted this particular ferry terminal and have even been known to make the crossing.

The timetable will tell you whether the ferry is going to Unst or to Fetlar and if you are taking a car it is wise to book by telephoning the booking office at Burravoe (Tel: 01957 722 259).

The ferry crossing to Unst takes about ten minutes and no matter what the weather it is worth standing out on deck as the boat passes Linga on its starboard side and you can enjoy an uninterrupted view to port up the Blue Mull sound.

You never know what you might see. The P&O ferry, the St. Clair has sailed through Blue Mull Sound. It was swum for the first recorded time by Dr. Richard Pike, a BP engineer at Sullom Voe Terminal in 1980 following his successful swim of Yell Sound. Richard Harmer of Yell also swam Blue Mull Sound later in 1980. You may spot seals, dolphins or even a whale and usually flocks of seabirds in a hurry.

Belmont has no facilities other than toilets and telephone. A salmon cage is sited near the pier and otters are often seen swimming in the bay. Geologists may be tempted to explore the quarry at the rear of the car park.

A NOTE ON SOME HISTORICAL ACCOUNTS OF UNST

Unst was the island that provided the nearest and safest landfall for the Viking settlers in the 8th century and it has been suggested that the name was "Onest" – in Norse meaning "the island nearest" as it was and still is, to Norway.

Human habitation, however, existed for centuries before the Vikings came and Petester above the west shore of the Loch of Cliff is thought to have been the seter (pasture) of the Picts. The Picts are also thought to have built at least nine brochs in Unst, the greatest of the survivors being Snabrough, 63½ft.

Christianity was probably introduced to the Picts by 7th century Celtic missionaries of the Columbian tradition and a reminder of their dwelling in Unst is in the place name Papil (Papa = father). In medieval times up to fourteen chapels were established, two of them with dedications to Norse saints St. Olaf and St. Sunniva, indicating the christianisation of the Vikings. Three sites compete for the honour of being the ting or Norse parliament site mentioned in the Orkneyinga saga: at Crussafield's circles of stones, at Gunnister's scalloped stone and by the ruined kirk at Baliasta.

Muness Castle, built in the 16th century, is the building which is a reminder of the transition from the Norse heritage to the Scottish feudal system. However, trade continued to be international with the Dutch dominating the fish trade and there are two Hanseatic merchants buried at Lund. The population peaked in 1861 at 3060 and many people emigrated during the later part of that century. The herring industry 1880-1925 created a lot of activity during the fishing season but it was hosiery and the development of the mineral industry which, with employment by the Shetland Islands Council and crofting, provided the most stable forms of occupation.

The establishment of RAF Saxa Vord, the development of tourism and the role which Baltasound Airport had in the development and operations of the East Shetland Basin oil fields have all contributed to Unst's economy in recent years. Today it is the salmon hatcheries and fish farms which are of increasing importance with other initiatives in tourism and small business development.

A NOTE ON SOME HISTORICAL ACCOUNTS OF UNST

Previous visitors who have written a description of Unst described it as follows:

John Brand (1701) reported, "… it is said to be the largest pleasant isle in all this Country".

Thomas Gifford (1733) found, "… the inhabitants are for the most part fishers. They have oxen, cows, some sheep, and plenty of little horses".

George Low (1774) delights that, "Otters very numerous and large about Unst; I measured one in a gentleman's house which was 59 inches from the nose to the tail". After Christmas he found that the people, "meet in considerable numbers, men and women, and divert themselves in playing at cards etc. *till the night is well spent.*" Times don't change!

Samuel Hibbert (1822) found the 'Burn of Health'. "Among the serpentine hills, which in quest of the chromate of iron, I took much labour in exploring, there is a pure stream that has long been celebrated for its supposed sanative virtues". However, he is advised that, "… the influence of the water god has long been on the wane".

Christian Ployen (1840) the Danish Governor of the Faroes. It took ten and half hours to row him from Bressay to Belmont: "I was very glad when at last I sat at Belmont by a cheerful fireside, which was pleasant, although it was the 24th July".

John Reid (1869) began his art ramble in Unst by landing at Uyeasound, "… and in company with a party of gentlemen, walked over the hills to Balta, a distance of six miles". Walking was no easy task, "… generally speaking, it is literally a 'hop, step and jump'".

Dr. Robert Cowie (1871) quotes Biot the French philosopher's comments, in 1817: "If there were only trees and sun, no residence could be more pleasant; but if there were trees and sun, everybody would wish to go thither, and peace would exist no longer". Cowie would not have enjoyed the Round Unst Trek for he considered, "There is nothing worthy of remark on the bold and rocky West Coast of Unst".

John Tudor (1883) was a walker. "Like the southern half of the island, the northern may be divided into two pedestrian excursions". If, "… the whole round including Colvidale and the Blue Mull is rather too much for one walk the route home from the Blue Mull might be varied by passing through the haaf-station at Newgord, and then along the Cliff line as far as the crest of Vallafield whence you can strike a bee-line for Balta Sound".

Dr. Mortimer Manson (1942) thought that: "The number and variety of interesting archaeological sites on the island of Unst should afford great attraction and give satisfaction to visitors who are interested in antiquarian pursuits".

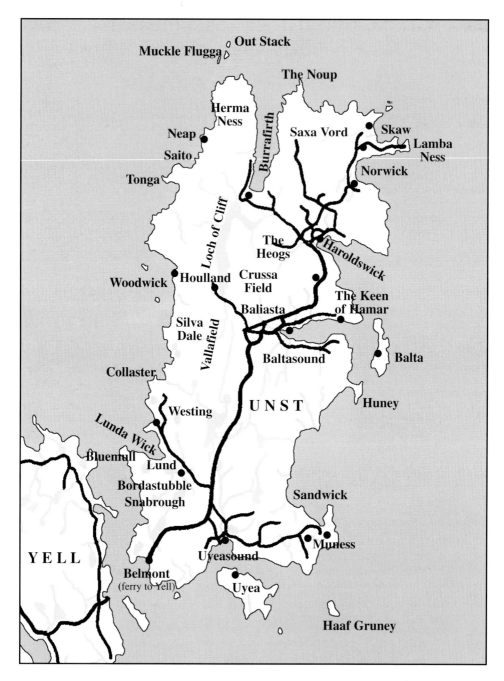

Muckle Flugga Out Stack

The Noup

Herma Ness

Burrafirth

Saxa Vord Skaw

Neap

Lamba Ness

Saito

Norwick

Tonga

Loch of Cliff

The Heogs

Haroldswick

Woodwick Houlland Crussa Field

The Keen of Hamar

Baliasta

Silva Dale

Vallafield

Baltasound Balta

Collaster

U N S T Huney

Westing

Lunda Wick

Bluemull Lund

Bordastubble
Snabrough Sandwick

YELL Uyeasound Muness

Belmont
(ferry to Yell) Uyea

Haaf Gruney

The Island of Unst showing start and finishing points of sections of the Round Unst Trek, cross-country walks and the Islands of Balta and Uyea.

■■■ WALKING THE COASTLINE OF SHETLAND NO. 2 ■■■
THE ISLAND OF UNST

60 Miles (100 Kilometres)

ROUND UNST TREK

Section	From	To	Miles	(Kms)	Hrs	Page
1	BELMONT	WESTING	6.5	11	4	15
2	WESTING	WOODWICK	4.5	7.5	2.5	21
3	WOODWICK	HERMANESS	6	10	3	26
4	HERMANESS	BURRAFIRTH	8	13	4	31
5	BURRAFIRTH	SKAW	7	11.5	4	34
6	SKAW	NORWICK	3	5	2	38
7	NORWICK	HAROLDSWICK	4	6.5	2	43
8	HAROLDSWICK	BALTASOUND	4.5	7.5	2	49
9	BALTASOUND	MUNESS	8.5	14	4	55
10	MUNESS	UYEASOUND	5	8	2	60
11	UYEASOUND	BELMONT	3	5	2	63
		TOTAL	**60**	**100**	**31**	

CROSS COUNTRY AND CIRCULAR WALKS

Section	From	To	Miles	(Kms)	Hrs	Page
A	BELMONT	Snabrough	4.5	7.5	2.5	64
B	BORDASTUBBLE	Lunda Wick	3	5	2.5	66
C	WESTING BEACH	Silva Dale	6	10	4	71
D	HOULLAND	Woodwick	3	5	2	72
E	HERMANESS		8	13	4	75
F	SKAW		6	10	3-4	79
G	LAMBA NESS		3	5	2	82
H	THE HEOGS, NIKKA VORD AND CRUSSA FIELD		4	6.5	2	84
I	THE KEEN OF HAMAR		2	3	2	87
J	SANDWICK AND MUNESS CASTLE		5	8	3	90
K	BELMONT	Uyeasound	5	8	3	93
L	UYEA ISLE		5	8	3	95
M	BALTA ISLAND		4	6	2	99

Maps: Ordnance Survey Landranger 1 Shetland: Yell and Unst
1:50,000 1.5 in to 1 mile 2 cm to 1 km.
For greater detail use Pathfinder series
1: 25,000
Sheet HU 59/69 Fetlar (North) Pathfinder 4
        HP 40/50/60 Baltasound
        HP 51/61 Haroldswick
Geological map of Scotland (Institute of Geological Services)
Northern Shetland Sheets 129, 130 and 131

SAFETY AND CONSERVATION

Be prepared.

Have a knowledge of basic First Aid.

Know how to navigate properly using map and compass.

Carry the Ordnance Survey (OS) maps appropriate to the walk.

Select the right equipment for walking. Carry waterproofs, spare sweater, whistle, food, torch, gloves and balaclava. A mobile telephone is now considered an essential accessory by some walkers but it may not register a signal in parts of Unst.

Leave word of your planned walk and report your return.

Respect the land.

Take care not to drop litter. It is unsightly and can be dangerous to animals.

Remember to use gates or stiles where possible instead of climbing fences and walls.

Park with consideration, remembering that agricultural vehicles may need access near where you leave a car.

Keep dogs under full control. Remember crofters are entitled to shoot dogs worrying sheep.

Be weatherwise.

Exercise caution in low cloud or mist.

On cliffs windy and misty conditions can create dangerous situations.

Aim to complete a walk in daylight hours.

WALK 1: BELMONT – WESTING ▓▓▓▓▓▓▓▓▓▓▓

6½ miles (11 kms) : 4 hours

OS Maps: Landranger Sheet 1 Shetland – Yell & Unst
Pathfinder Sheet HP 40/50/60 Baltasound

Car pick-up point – At road end, The Booth, Westing Beach

Belmont is the Unst ferry terminal and start point for a walk which is a great introduction to the island. Before you have walked very far you will pass, to the right on the hill above you, a partially excavated early Viking Longhouse. By way of contrast the view in front is dominated by Belmont House which was built in 1775 by Thomas Mouat. Once described as "the most ambitious classical house in the northern isles" and at one time the home of Major Cameron, the Laird of the Garth Estate. The house has been virtually uninhabited since 1914. The deterioration of this fine building has lead to the establishment of the Belmont Trust which aims to restore it (Tel: 01595 820281). Apart from a stiff climb up to the top of Blue Mull headland this walk is on the green tops of the low lying cliffs containing few hazards.

Leave the car park and walk up the main road past the old jetty and sign warning drivers to watch out for ponies. A herd of Shetland ponies is often to be found here. Turn left down onto the beach and walk round the Wick of Belmont past a ruined power cable land fall. Because Fetlar fills the view to the south, it is like walking round a large lake. The path along the cliff edge is very narrow so you may prefer to walk along the beach. At Hoga Ness is the magnificent ruin of a broch. Originally thought to have been a building with an overall diameter of about 60ft and a wall thickness of 15ft the surround's defences can still be clearly followed. The ramparts are massive and the ditches deep and in places cut through rock. Of special note is the stone-faced inner rampart to the North East of the broch which is at least 10ft thick. A ruined building stands within it.

The walk is on grass and easy going. To the right are the remains of a small house, croft ruins and a cairn of stones collected from

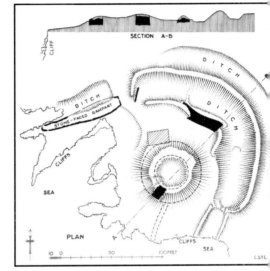

Hoga Ness Broch, Belmont.

cultivated areas. Across the Sound much of Cullivoe is visible, including the Church of St. Olaf. A recent power cable landfall is marked and the cable itself can be seen like a serpent under the water at a pebbly beach.

Turn into the sheltered bay at Snarra Voe with power cable signs both sides of the voe. With the ruins of Voeside on the shore and the ruined crofting township visible on higher ground, the place has a desolate air. It must have been quite different when the ferry to Yell used to cross from here, though John Reid, in 1867, said of the crossing, "… the tides are so strong, that, with an insufficient crew (he'd employed "two frail fishermen and a youth") there is a risk of being carried out to sea. Looking over the boat's side you can scarcely persuade yourself that the

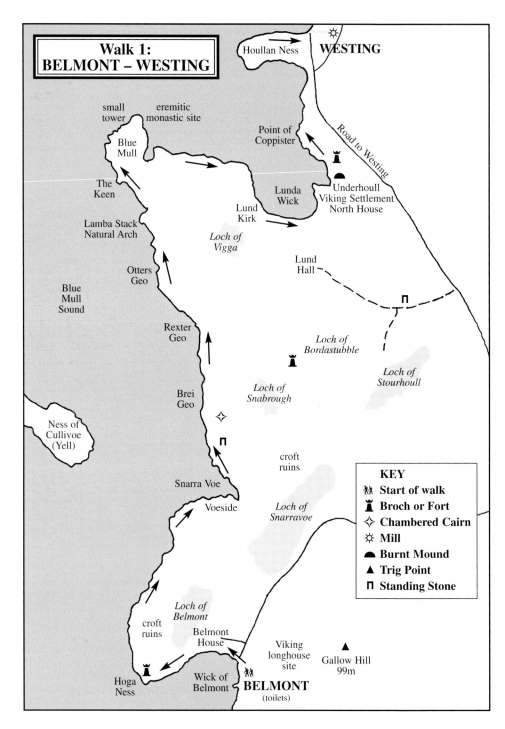

Walk 1:
BELMONT – WESTING

Houllan Ness

WESTING

small tower

eremitic monastic site

Blue Mull

Point of Coppister

Road to Westing

The Keen

Lunda Wick

Underhoull Viking Settlement North House

Lund Kirk

Lamba Stack Natural Arch

Loch of Vigga

Lund Hall

Otters Geo

Π

Blue Mull Sound

Rexter Geo

Loch of Bordastubble

Loch of Stourhoull

Brei Geo

Loch of Snabrough

Ness of Cullivoe (Yell)

Π

croft ruins

Snarra Voe

KEY

Voeside

Loch of Snarravoe

🚶 **Start of walk**

🏰 **Broch or Fort**

✧ **Chambered Cairn**

☼ **Mill**

⬣ **Burnt Mound**

▲ **Trig Point**

Π **Standing Stone**

Loch of Belmont

croft ruins

Belmont House

Viking longhouse site

Gallow Hill 99m

Hoga Ness

Wick of Belmont

BELMONT (toilets)

16

Sound is not boiling, so exactly does the simmering motion resemble the surface of boiling water".

It was from here that on the 22nd May, 1856, Grace Petrie and her sister-in-law, Helen, rowed out into a storm-tossed Blue Mull sound with her 79 year old father-in-law, James, at the helm to rescue two men from drowning.

Grace had spotted an upturned boat with two men clinging to the keel being swept past Snarravoe before a northerly gale and insisted on a rescue mission.

On reaching the wreck the two women dragged John Spence, a merchant of Westing, and his assistant Laurence Jamieson, to safety. A third man, John Thomson had, sadly, been swept away by the tide and drowned when the flit boat capsized on its way from Uyeasound to Westing.

Grace, "Shetland's Grace Darling", was later awarded the Royal Humane Society's medal

and lived on to 98 years of age. Helen was also honoured in Unst and was presented with a Bible by the parishioners.

There is a ruined booth on the foreshore and the whole area is very marshy. The snipe and heron enjoy it but it is best to walk the water edge. Proceeding north we pass a stone wall, 150ft long and carefully built, presumably as a sheep shelter. After this is an enclosure with a standing stone 4ft high, not unlike that at Gutcher which, with binoculars, can be seen from this spot.

After crossing a wire fence divert briefly to climb east up to a prominent knoll on which stands the substantial ruins of a cairn with magnificent views.

Pass a ruined enclosure above a beach upon which a small grass covered stack defiantly survives. Below the cliffs some flat stones will come into view after which the ground starts to rise. At beautiful Rexter Geo admire a cove with the features of a miniature harbour

Lamba Stack.

The Keen at Blue Mull.

complete with blue green sea and natural arches. There are caves at Otters Geo and double natural arches on Lamba Stack to be viewed from a plateau before the final haul up to the Blue Mull itself.

Entrance is gained by passing through a wall which stands like a ghostly battlement of a long ago fort. At the NW end of the Mull itself there is a tiny stone wall – 6ft long x 3ft high and below this is a small tower 30ft round and 6ft high at the northern side. Remains of watch towers? Certainly a superb place to view the coastline of North Yell to the west and the west coast of Unst. The 'Inventory' notes that on the extremity of this headland are seven small oval mounds close together which may have prehistoric origins and according to Noel Fojut could be the remains of an eremitic monastic site.

Leave Blue Mull by steep descent on eastern side through the northern end of the 'battlement' wall and follow the coast round to Lunda Wick. Across the bay opposite can be

seen the Viking settlement of Underhoull on the slope below and to the right of a broch mound. The ruined, roofless 12th century church of Lunda Wick, St. Olafs, measures 47ft 5in by 22ft 2ins and stands in a graveyard. The fact that the church is so small, as all the medieval churches are here, would indicate, it has been suggested by Sam Polson, a small population, for in those days attendance would have been compulsory. The entrance is in the centre of the west gable and within is an unusual carving of a fish on the underside of the top lintel of the SE window.

Also inside is one of the two tombs of Bremen merchants buried at Lund, their tombstones carved with inscriptions in Low German. "Here lies the worthy Segebad Detken, burgess and merchant of Bremen. He carried on his business in this country of 52 years and fell blissfully asleep in our Lord in the year 1573 on the 20th of August. God rest his soul". The other slab lies immediately east of the church and shows three shields and the inscription: "In the year 1585 on the 25th July, being St. James's day, the worthy and well born Henrick Segelcken the elder, from Germany, and a burgess of the town Bremen, fell asleep here in God the Lord. May God be gracious to him".

The graveyard has an area dedicated to the Sandison family and dominating the memorials is one in red marble to Alexander of Lund who died in 1900, "greatly beloved. Full of Grace and Power".

By way of contrast, to the south of the church are eight headstones in the form of rude stone crosses. But the memorial that few miss is opposite the entrance and carries the message from, presumably the young, Peter Bruce Harper who died in 1854:

> *Weep Not For Me, My Parents Dear,*
> *I Am Not Dead, But Sleeping Here.*
> *My Glass Is Run, My Grave You See*
> *Be Shure, Prepare, To Follow Me*
> *TIME FLYS!*

Cross the beach at Lund beneath the staring ruin of Lund Hall unless you are returning to Belmont in which case turn to Circular Walk A page 64.

The hall was built in the early 18th century and should not be investigated too closely as the structure is very dangerous; the roof was removed in 1947. According to Jessie Saxby a hated laird dressed up an accomplice to look like a devil and sent him into Lund Kirk during a service. This caused the congregation considerable alarm. So upset was the minister that, quoting scripture as his authority, he cursed the laird. No service was held in that kirk again and the laird's land fell into other hands and his name has perished. There is also a legend concerning a visit by Lucifer himself to the hall one Yule and leaving behind the imprint of a hoof in one of the flagstones. Certainly not a place to dally.

Round the bay to walk beneath Iron Age and

Lund Kirk and Lunda Wick. Lund Hall on the hill above.

Norse farmstead sites at Underhoull. It is worth exploring the ruins of the early 9th century Norse houses excavated in the 1960s. A boat shaped Norse longhouse has been constructed from earlier Iron Age round houses on the same site. The whole site now is sadly falling into disrepair but there is enough to give one some sense of the settlement.

Above the Norse farmstead is the Broch of Underhoull which, though ruined, is impressive. Extensive defensive ramparts of earth, with an intervening ditch, protected the broch, the approach to which was by causeway from the north west. There is a display of Viking artefacts found at Underhoull in the Shetland Museum.

You are less than 100 yards from the road so may be tempted to follow the road down to Point of Coppister. Here the coast may be resumed round Houllan Ness to the Burn of Bighton on the pebbly beach of Westing. By a restored old booth there is just room at the road end to turn round a car if leaving the coast at this point.

If time allows it is worth visiting a restored water mill by following the Burn of Bighton up towards the road leading to the main settlement area of Westing. The mill will be found before the burn disappears under the road.

Shetland water mill.

WALK 2: WESTING – WOODWICK

4½ miles (7½ kms) : 2½ hours

OS Maps: Landranger Sheet 1 Shetland – Yell & Unst
Pathfinder Sheet HP 40/50/60 Baltasound
HP 51/61 Haroldswick

Nearest car pick-up point to Woodwick is Houlland (6 miles [9 kms]) : 3½ hours

Westing beach is a good place to spot otters but other attractions await along this stretch of coastline which is easy going, apart from a narrow pathway on the climb up from Hagdales Nest. The deserted crofting area of Collaster and the waterfalls at impressive Longa Geo are notable and you may choose to take a break at the ruined crofthouse at Clave.

Cross above the pebbly beach to walk past a self-catering cottage on the sea shore. The

islands of Brough Holm, Round Holm and Lang Holm lie just offshore. There are the remains of a broch on Brough Holm which is about ¼ mile from the shore. This broch was surrounded by a massive defensive wall up to 10ft thick. Outside the wall is a ditch and beyond this a rampart of earth and stones. The sea has swept away some of the main structure along with the rocky face on which it stood. Evidently the Laird of Lund built a booth on the island with stones from the broch and the stones were used

Woodwick.

21

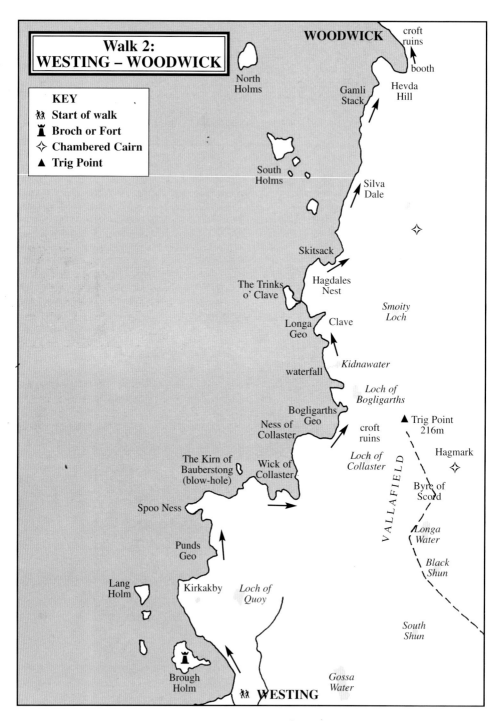

Walk 2:
WESTING – WOODWICK

KEY
🚶 **Start of walk**
♟ **Broch or Fort**
✧ **Chambered Cairn**
▲ **Trig Point**

WOODWICK

croft ruins

booth

North Holms

Gamli Stack

Hevda Hill

South Holms

Silva Dale

✧

Skitsack

The Trinks o' Clave

Hagdales Nest

Smoity Loch

Longa Geo

Clave

waterfall

Kidnawater

Loch of Bogligarths

Bogligarths Geo

▲ Trig Point 216m

Ness of Collaster

croft ruins

Loch of Collaster

Hagmark

✧

The Kirn of Bauberstong (blow-hole)

Wick of Collaster

V A L L A F I E L D

Byre of Scord

Spoo Ness

Longa Water

Black Shun

Punds Geo

Lang Holm

Kirkakby

Loch of Quoy

South Shun

♟

Brough Holm

🚶 WESTING

Gossa Water

as ballast by fishing boats. Nobody suggests that the broch was accessible from the shore at low water. As one rounds the North Sound there are superb views of Blue Mull and North Yell and from Kirkaby, Gloup Holm is visible. Pass stone clearance cairns on the approach to ruined remains of Kirkaby Church situated on a small mound opposite Lang Holm. The foundations are barely visible and with other buildings sharing the site it is difficult to confirm what was what. An 1863 plan describes a 14ft x 12ft nave and 10ft x 7ft chancel.

Round Punds Geo the going can be wet as one climbs above the rocky foreshore onto a plateau overlooked by a navigational aid in the shape of a small 'golf-ball' on top of Byre of Scord. Cross a fence to aim for Spoo Ness where seals may be seen basking. Cross a burn and fence to reach pebbly beach at Wick of Collaster. At the Ayre of Collaster a blow hole, 'The Kirn of Bauberstong' may be observed in action. Note extensive croft ruins on the slopes to the east. There are four noosts at the wick and planticrus, but I have not found a mill though the area is marshy and the burn fast flowing. There is a track from the settlement over a stone bridge going south towards Westing. Pass a small cluster of standing stones and admire the many geos and waterfalls along this particular stretch of coastline, particularly Bogligarth's Geo below the Loch of Bogligarth and Longa Geo. Near Hagdales Ness is a ruined croft at Clave

and a natural mound catches one's attention. If the roar of the sea can be heard it is probably caused by it meeting The Trinks o'Clave.

At Skitsack the island of South Holms is visible. Climb into the hill over a fence and onto the slopes of Silva Dale. There is an evil green burn to be crossed before one enjoys a superb view of a subterranean passage through South Holms Island. One is now walking on a slope; descend to cross a burn and climb to a fence on slopes of Hevda Hill. There is a good view north of Sneuga Hill as one descends into Wood Wick. Before reaching the beach note the terrain above the northern shore and plan to go north by climbing round the Ward of Petester rather than attempting to get round the crags on the coastline.

Cross the burn which has flowed down the Dale of Woodwick (up which you can escape to the road at Houlland above the Loch of Cliff if you wish to leave the coastline at this point (1½ miles : [2½ kms]) – next easy exit is not until Milldale Burn at Ayre of Tonga).

Woodwick is aptly named and there are some derelict stone fishing booths and a noost. Hibbert thought it a place "… interesting to the mineralogist by the crystals of granitite which are so abundantly diffused throughout its rocks".

INTRODUCTION TO THE LAND OF THE GIANTS ■

Before venturing further north it will be useful to give some background information on Herma Ness and Saxa Vord, two land masses separated by the waters of Burrafirth. Neither should be explored without carrying compass, small torch, whistle and other useful emergency items. Fog is the main threat so it is well worthwhile taking safety precautions.

Frank Renwick in his book 'Noost' describes the adventures of a party lost on Hermaness. "They got up eventually and went in a northerly direction. But the mist did not give way to gentle sunshine as the clergy man had foretold. It thickened till the party was caught up in it like a swirling flannel cloak and could barely see each other. It wasn't only thick, it was cold and very wet …". So be prepared for fog and in winter for gale force winds, which have been known, as on New Years Eve 1991, to reach 200mph, with tragic results.

Hermaness, Burrafirth and Loch of Cliff from Saxa Vord.

INTRODUCTION TO THE LAND OF THE GIANTS

Herma Ness, 657ft (200m) and Saxa Vord 935ft (280m) are both named after Norse giants who once lived in the areas of Unst named after them. Jessie Saxby relates that Saxa was a rough, blustering fellow fond of fighting and eating. Herman on the other hand was a placid, poetical giant who liked to be out on the hillside and a friend of the local community.

One day Herman and Saxa fell in love with the mermaid, Utsta (Outstack) who, whilst not attracted to either of them, could not resist the chance of flirting with the two giants. During the day she reclined on the south side of the isle for Saxa's benefit and in the evening the 'piscatorial coquette' moved to the north of the isle to excite Herman's interest. Eventually jealousy drove the giants to fight but whilst they were throwing boulders at each other a witch became so cross she flung a shroud of green turf over Saxa so that he was buried on Saxa Vord. Herman she changed into a wreath of mist and this is likely to be found on Herma Ness at any time. It has been suggested that Herman and Saxa may not have been Norse but Saxon and certainly the names have a Germanic ring. Perhaps they briefly ruled the island before they or their descendants were overcome by the Viking invaders.

Today Hermaness is a National Nature Reserve. The nests of over 650 breeding pairs of great skuas (bonxies) are to be found on the reserve and care must be taken to avoid walking on their eggs or chicks. At the height of the nesting season the bonxie will attack people walking near their ground nesting sites by swooping on them with wings outstretched and webbed feet down, like an aircraft undercarriage. It's their feet which can catch your head. If you don't have a stick it can help to walk with one arm raised in the air to ward off such low level 'buzzing' attacks. The wailing shriek of the arctic skua (aalin) may also be heard in contrast to the pre-emptory croak of the bonxie.

Sir Walter Scott must have had the cliffs or North Unst in mind when he wrote:

> *"Here rise no groves, and here no gardens blow,*
> *Here even the hardy heath scarce dares to grow;*
> *But rocks on rocks, in mist and storm array'd,*
> *Stretch far to sea their giant colonnade,*
> *With many a cavern seam'd, the dreary haunt*
> *Of the dun seal and swarthy cormorant,*
> *Wild, round their rufted brows with frequent cry,*
> *As of lament, the gulls and gannets fly,*
> *And from their sable base, with sullen sound,*
> *In sheets of whitening foam the waves rebound".*

Like so much of Scott's works this passage is best spoken aloud, slowly and in as deep a voice as possible!

WALK 3: WOODWICK – HERMANESS (NEAP) ████████████

6 miles (10 kms) : 3 hours

OS Maps: Landranger Sheet 1 Shetland – Yell & Unst
Pathfinder Sheet HP 51/61 Haroldswick

Car access point – Houlland 1½ miles (2½ kms)
Car pick-up point – Burrafirth (8 miles [13 kms]) : 4 hours

Woodwick – Burrafirth including Herma Ness (combining walks 3 & 4) is 11 miles (17½ kms). Allow 6 hours as there is a lot to see and it becomes a bit of a slog at the end.

Good cliff walking with various attractions including The Geo of Brough, Goturm's Hole and the sight of Ayre of Tonga. Short climbs at Woodwick, Libbers Hill and Tonga. This section ends near Neap where the 170 meters

high cliffs of Hermaness National Nature Reserve are home to over 100,000 breeding sea birds.

After climbing up from Woodwick towards Ward of Petester visit extensive croft ruins and rejoin the coastline north of Skate Stack opposite North Holms islands. Above Valaberg cross a burn into the massive stone enclosure surrounding South Geo of Brough of Flubersgerdie. At a white outcrop Tonga comes into view to the north.

On the Taing of Brough, the promontory between the creeks of North and South Geo of Brough, Dr. Lamb has identified the site of an iron age promontory fort. Access is by a very narrow neck and at the far end are the remains of a stone and turf enclosure measuring roughly 15ft by 12ft. On the plateau behind it are large stone boulders and a very large stone enclosure. Perhaps this massive enclosure was for the protection of the inhabitants and their stock with the promontory fort being the last redoubt? Continue north noting the sea boiling over South Croga Skerry before rounding the coast to Greff at the foot of Libbers Hill (170m). Pass a ruined water mill and begin the ascent with red cliffs of Tonga in view. Keep near to wire fence and withstand chuckles of fulmars watching your slow progress. Catch breath by admiring view south over the Lochs of North Water and Heimar Water to distant Byre of Scord. On the top make your way round a fissure on cliff edge (once I discovered the home of a large, ugly, feral cat) to cross a fence and follow a fence over a burn.

Where the fence begins a steep descent down to the stone wall at Ayre of Tonga in the valley Goturm's Hole is clearly marked on the OS

South Geo
of Brough

North Geo
of Brough

0   m   20
0 —————— 50 ft

Taing of Brough, Flubersgerdie. The path approaches across a narrow saddle. Two-thirds up the steep slope there are the remains of a stone wall. On the summit is a very hummocky area with projecting stones.

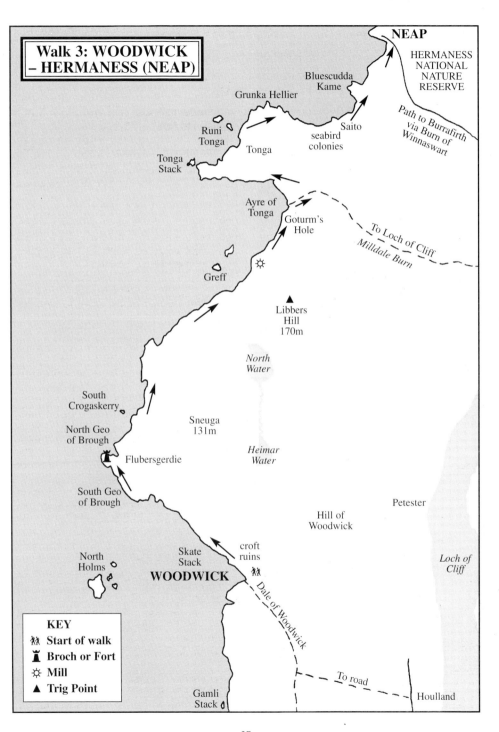

Walk 3: WOODWICK – HERMANESS (NEAP)

NEAP

HERMANESS
NATIONAL
NATURE
RESERVE

Bluescudda
Kame

Grunka Hellier

Path to Burrafirth via Burn of Winnaswart

Runi
Tonga

Saito
seabird
colonies

Tonga

Tonga
Stack

Ayre of
Tonga

Goturm's
Hole

To Loch of Cliff

Milldale Burn

Greff

▲
Libbers
Hill
170m

*North
Water*

South
Crogaskerry

Sneuga
131m

North Geo
of Brough

*Heimar
Water*

Flubersgerdie

South Geo
of Brough

Petester

Hill of
Woodwick

*Loch of
Cliff*

North
Holms

Skate
Stack

croft
ruins

WOODWICK

Dale of Woodwick

Gamli
Stack

To road

Houlland

KEY
🚶 **Start of walk**
♟ **Broch or Fort**
☼ **Mill**
▲ **Trig Point**

map. Finding it is a different thing altogether and there is a danger that realisation of one's success in determining its location might only occur as one plunges out of sight 50 feet down a chute into a large cave below. It necessitates climbing over the wire fence as it descends steeply down the cliff edge towards the Ayre of Tonga. The only other route to the cave is by climbing 200 feet up the precipitous cliffs from the sea shore. Climbing over the wire fence to examine the hole on the cliff edge more closely is not recommended in windy weather.

Goturm was a Viking raider who plundered Unst regularly until, to the islanders' hearty relief, his ship was wrecked on the Holm of Woodwick. Unfortunately, they were dismayed to discover, not only was Goturm the sole survivor but also he had managed to get ashore and obtain shelter and safe sanctuary in the cave high up the cliffs.

It was earnestly hoped that he would starve to death there but, contrary to expectation, he managed to endure his ordeal somehow, and one day was discovered to have gone from the cave and escaped from the island altogether. Several months later a longship flying his standard was sighted off Unst and the folk trembled as they awaited some terrible form of retribution. Goturm, however, came not to raid

Left and below: Goturm's Hole.

but brought gifts. He admitted that he owed his survival in Unst and the means of his escape to some local girls, the daughters of Kender, who had taken pity on him and had lowered provisions and fuel down through the hole to the cave below. When their father, Maunce Kender, saw the costly gifts he is reported to have immediately forgiven his daughters and murmured: "The deil is aye kind till his ain" (the devil looks after his own).

The descent to the valley is not best made from here. Traverse the slope higher up until an easier descent can be made. Follow the burn on the north side away from the Ayre and its stone wall until the valley widens out at two mounds. Turn north and climb onto Tonga. Saxa Vord and Muckle Flugga come into view.

Aim to traverse Tonga to Runi Tonga and then walk north until looking over Grunka Hellier, for here the view of Muckle Flugga can be fully appreciated. There is a small stone cairn. Descend to follow coastline round to Saito. As one leaves Tonga pass a withered wooden pole on the edge of the cliff which has been of considerable assistance to me when caught in a mist in the area. There are small tarns inland but it is the cliffs below which attract the eye as in the summer many puffins and gannets are to be seen here in addition to the all the year round resident fulmars. At the height of the breeding season the sound of all the different birds at their different levels on the sheer cliffs of Saito and Bluescudda Kame is one never to be forgotten.

Saito, Hermaness. Favourite cliff edge to look down on 'Albert Ross'.

On the cliff tops the puffins will be found either sitting outside their burrows or, like mechanical toys, taking off for the sea below or returning from it carrying sand eels. There is no guarantee that you will see any great number and quite often it appears that the whole puffin colony has gone fishing. The fulmars will be about, though, and the gannets – at the granite cliff of Saito it is possible to look down on their nests quite safely and without disturbing the birds.

Between 1972 and 1987 a solitary black-browed albatross lived with the gannet colony. 'Albert Ross' arrived with the gannets each spring (February 14th was the earliest sighting) and left with them to return offshore each autumn. Albert had no mate but for 15 years enjoyed his visits to Unst and was one of the most photographed birds in Shetland during those years. In 1990 he made a dramatic return to Saito but he has not been seen since 1995. Below the gannets are the kittiwakes, guillemots and razorbills.

From Bluescudda Kame follow the cliff edge round Neap where you can choose to pick up the Hermaness National Nature Reserve waymarked path which heads SE to Burn of Winnaswarta and then S to the car park above the former Muckle Flugga shore station.

The shore station, site of the 'Root Stacks Hotel' in Hammond Innes's novel 'North Star' (1974) has now been converted into private flats. Scottish Natural Heritage, steward of the reserve, has a visitor centre and a summer warden is based here.

'Albert Ross' kept the gannets in order.

WALK 4: HERMANESS (NEAP) – BURRAFIRTH

8 miles (13 kms) : 4 hours

OS Maps: **Landranger Sheet 1 Shetland – Yell & Unst**
Pathfinder Sheet HP 51/61 Haroldswick

Car access point – Hermaness car park, Burrafirth

This is a most exciting stretch of the Unst coastline and will include walking cliffs between 200 and 500 feet high but the terrain is never difficult. During the sea-bird breeding season the puffin colonies are particularly enjoyable. Beware the bonxies and be prepared for a bit of a slog over the moor to complete this walk.

'Watch your feet' will be important safety advice to remember as one walks north, with the eye constantly being attracted to either follow the flight of birds, or admire the actions of the waves on the many and varied stacks. Tooa marks the start of the array of stacks which can be viewed from Toolie before the descent to East Sothers Dale which can be reasonably sheltered. Ascend round the lower slopes of Hermaness Hill, where more stacks begin at Flodda, to Boelie where a track once used by the lighthouse men comes directly from

Burrafirth over the top of Hermaness Hill (trig point 657ft/200m). The ruined arms of the old signalling station, which used to be operated on a daily basis by a lighthouse keeper on shore duty, once were used to send messages to the lighthouse. In 1939 a radio transmitter/receiver was installed, a development which probably cheered all the keepers, on or offshore, immensely.

One can walk out onto a stretch of land like the flight deck of an aircraft carrier at Wilna Geo and be as close as one can be, on land, to Muckle Flugga, Little Flugga and the various Skerries around it and of course Out Stack, which is best viewed from Gord. Most of the larger stacks show evidence of considerable bird activity, particularly gannets.

After all this excitement it can be rather an anticlimax to walk the east cliffs of Hermaness

Puffins discuss walkers on the cliffs of Hermaness.

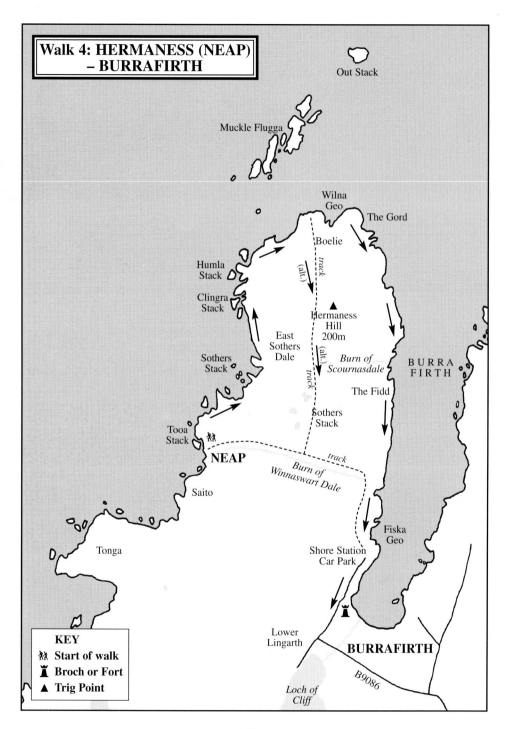

Walk 4: HERMANESS (NEAP) – BURRAFIRTH

Out Stack

Muckle Flugga

Wilna Geo

The Gord

Boelie

Humla Stack

track

(alt.)

Clingra Stack

▲ Hermaness Hill 200m

East Sothers Dale

(alt.)

track

Burn of Scournasdale

BURRA FIRTH

Sothers Stack

The Fidd

Sothers Stack

Tooa Stack

NEAP

track

Burn of Winnaswart Dale

Saito

Fiska Geo

Tonga

Shore Station Car Park

Lower Lingarth

BURRAFIRTH

B9086

KEY
👫 Start of walk
⌘ Broch or Fort
▲ Trig Point

Loch of Cliff

32

and the going can get tiresome particularly from the Burn of Scournasdale if there has been wet weather. The views across Burra Firth of Saxa Vord can however afford some compensation but there is little bird activity.

You may feel like returning to Boelie and returning on the old route to the lighthouse shore station. It eventually connects with the SNH waymarked route on Hermaness Hill for the final descent to Burrafirth. From the car park follow the road down to the Burn of Burrafirth. You can visit the first recognised broch site since Underhoull by leaving the road on the left hand side and crossing a field down to a stile and onto a small rocky headland between Burgar Stack and where the Burn of Burrafirth flows into the sea. Under 60ft in diameter the broch is hidden beneath a grassy mound but many stones project through the turf. The mound was protected by one and possibly by two earthen ramparts on the landward side. It is a broch easily overlooked because in summer it is a place where the undergrowth survives to a height and disguises what is underneath. You may now choose, like one Frank Musgrave, to bivvy bag the night on Burrafirth beach.

Bonxies.

Landing supplies at Muckle Flugga by the *Grace Darling*, 1930s. In the boat (top to bottom) are Lowrie Edwardson, Willie Mathieson, Peter Sinclair and Tammy Edwardson. On the rocks (from left) are Willie Mathieson, Willie Mathieson, John Hughson, boatman, and John Spencer, lightkeeper.

WALK 5: BURRAFIRTH – SKAW

7 miles (11½ kms) : 4 hours

OS Maps: Landranger Sheet 1 Shetland – Yell & Unst
Pathfinder Sheet HP 51/61 Haroldswick

Car pick-up point – At road end at Skaw

The climb up the slopes of Saxa Vord is steep in parts but the reward is the experience of ever extensive, magnificent views. On rounding the point at The Noup the view is mainly of the hill which is probably just as well as there is an evil chasm to be avoided on the NE slope of Saxa Vord above Breiwick. This walk ends at the road outside Britain's most northerly house at Skaw.

From the Burn of Burra Firth take the road as far as the Buddabrake turning and follow the tarmac road towards this croft until a peat track appears going straight up the hill. Alternatively, cross the beach and make a way up below the fields of Buddabrake.

Climb up the hill in the direction of RAF Saxa Vord until a road which curves just below it is reached. Follow this road north and soon almost the whole of Muckle Flugga comes into view.

You may be tempted to climb to the top of Saxa Vord in which case make for the road which dog-legs up to the highest radar dome at 935ft (280m). There are fine and extensive views from the hill named in honour of the giant Saxa. A group of five large cairns was recorded in the Inventory of Shetland in 1946 but all traces of them seem to have disappeared. As did the first T80 radar, blown down by a severe gale in 1961. The replacement T80 was protected by a huge dome which remained until 1978.

"Afore da oil". Flitting Sydney and Barbara Priest's peats from Saxa Vord.

34

Vord is an Old Norse word for a heap of stones or cairn found on a mountain top and high hills which are often associated with watch towers. It is therefore appropriate that even today it is a place where the RAF keeps unending vigil for the security of the kingdom through the use of radar and fighter control. If one stands at the top site and listens to the wind whistling round the radome one is possibly reminded of Edgar in Shakespeare's 'King Lear' (and he knew a blasted heath or two) when he warns Oswald: "Keep out, che Vor or Ise try whether your costard or my ballow be the harder." The meaning is clear and over the years aerial visitors probing from the east have got the message. "The Condition upon which God hath

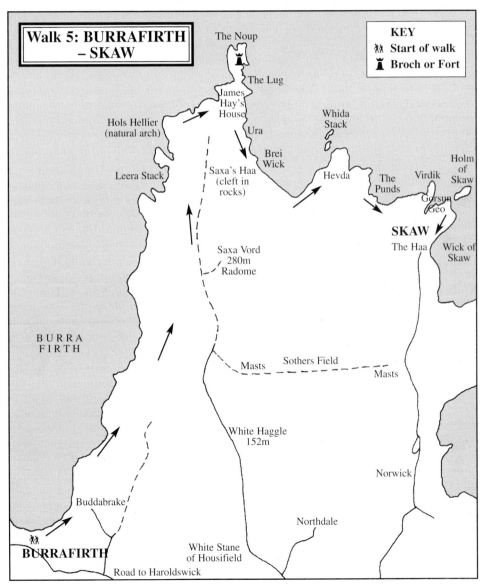

Walk 5: BURRAFIRTH – SKAW

KEY
ᛗᛗ **Start of walk**
🏛 **Broch or Fort**

The Noup

The Lug

James Hay's House

Hols Hellier (natural arch)

Ura

Whida Stack

Leera Stack

Brei Wick

Saxa's Haa (cleft in rocks)

Hevda

The Punds

Virdik

Holm of Skaw

Gorsun Geo

SKAW

Saxa Vord 280m Radome

The Haa

Wick of Skaw

BURRA FIRTH

Masts

Sothers Field

Masts

White Haggle 152m

Norwick

Buddabrake

ᛗᛗ
BURRAFIRTH

White Stane of Housifield

Northdale

Road to Haroldswick

Flugga light.

given liberty to a man," declaimed J. P. Curran in Dublin in 1790, "is eternal vigilance." Two hundred years later this is still the case but the future of the installation is under review.

Descend north towards Leera Stack on a bearing for the Out Stack past a concrete post. A road has been pushed out along the headland to allow maintenance to signal installations. The cliff scenery is dramatic where the sea has made great inroads to create natural arches and caves. You can take a canoe into many of the caves of Burra Firth. The only alarm I have ever experienced was once when I was in a two seat canoe and we found we were sharing the innermost part of a cave with a huge bull seal; there wasn't room for both canoe and seal. To this day I think we hold a record for back paddling.

Somehow the sheep even manage to climb the steepest land-connected stacks. The cliffs are up to 600ft in height and the natural arch of Hols Hellier has a bell-mounted entrance and is 170 yards long. It opens up into a mighty cave measuring 180ft broad and 30ft high.

The triangular shaped long narrow promontory of the Noup with its natural arch is a spectacular crag over 140m high and is the north eastern battlement of Unst. Dr Lamb identifies it as an Iron Age promontory fort site but having stayed

at cliff top level to admire it one then has a bit of a haul to climb up and around Brei Wick. In doing so one crosses the burn at Ura which attracted the interest of gold panner James Hay in the past. On the high plateau known as the "Croon o' da Ura" was once recorded a sort of natural broch and an underground room, known as Saxa's Haa. I have not found this but John Tudor (1883) writes that "Somewhere on Saxa Vord is a deep cleft in the rocks in which Saxa is reported to have dwelt when in the flesh." On a narrow plateau well up the hill above Breiwick there is an evil chasm within an area marked by four metal posts but no wire. I did look into the chasm as far as I dared and felt extremely uneasy but there was no sign of Saxa, 'in the flesh' or otherwise. It is an area of Unst which can stir all sorts of imaginings. In the cliff to the SE of Ura is a cave named "the trolls cave" so one may have to contend with them as well.

The Whida Stacks, like a pair of rugged twins, stand out off Hevda. Descend to climb Hill Ness where a stone wall built as a sheep shelter is a useful place for walkers to hide behind as well – it's about the only shelter to be found on this walk! Then from above Gorsun Geo turn round to view a final dramatic tableau of Muckle Flugga viewed through The Noup. A rocky 'claw' on top of the Lug is visible for the first time. Cross the slope diagonally over a fence to go towards the Holm of Skaw. Sheep are ferried across Ham Sound but the waters can be treacherous as the Russians found in 1967 when one of their spy trawlers was wrecked here. A wooden stile brings one over a fence above the lovely beach at Wick of Skaw. There are the remains of four noosts and three ancient round houses were just visible in the sand dunes of the cliffs a quarter of the way along the top.

In 1972 Ray Mitchell, a fireman at RAF Saxa Vord, and a team of enthusiastic amateur archaeologists carried out an excavation here following a discovery of several pieces of pottery and a stone club in the sand above the cliff face. Half of the buildings, dating back before the Norse period, had been lost over the cliff face due to natural erosion but more pottery, similar to that found on the Iron Age farmstead site at Clickimin, was found.

Mitchell thought that the sites his team excavated showed occupation levels of both the Bronze Age and the Iron Age. Certainly there are resemblances to other circular and oval dwellings which probably belong to the Iron Age and found in Caithness, Orkney and Shetland. There has not been much official recognition of this site and the closing words of Ray Mitchell's report reflect in some part his frustration:

"I have only scraped the surface of Skaw Valley, but I feel there is a wealth of information awaiting those who have the ability, interest and time to look into the past life of this Northernmost valley of the British Isles"

Unfortunately all traces of this site will shortly have eroded away.

Swimming can be enjoyed at Britain's most northerly beach. I was in a party of four which carried out a sponsored swim for the Red Cross here at noon on the shortest day 21st December 1975. The official time-keeper made us go back into the sea after we had nervously jumped the gun. It was like swimming in semi-set concrete and I was glad to survive both the swim and the drastic means of resuscitation afterwards.

Leave the beach across a slatted wooden bridge. The Haa of Skaw, Britain's most northerly house, lies at the end of the road.

Mid-winter solstice swim at Skaw for The Red Cross. Left to right: Chris Franklyn, Peter Guy, Andy Knill and Terry Dennett.

WALK 6: SKAW – NORWICK

3 miles (5 kms) : 2 hours

OS Maps: Landranger Sheet 1 Shetland – Yell & Unst
                Pathfinder Sheet HP 51/61 Haroldswick

A stroll round the NE corner of Unst with time to appreciate all that Lamba Ness has to offer – it is an excellent place to watch bird activity. Saxa's Kettle can be viewed before descending into the delightful bay at Norwick.

The Haa at Skaw, Britain's most northerly house, stands at the road end and is the start point for this walk. I have always thought that the road end at Skaw should have a sign which says, "The North – this is it." The millions of motorists who daily charge round the M25 and up M1, A1(M) or M6 are all advised that they are heading for 'The North'. Few can imagine what it is like at the actual road end of Skaw.

The upturned boat to the right of the house is a ship's lifeboat which now is seeing out its time as a shed roof. On the 20th October 1939 the *Sea Venture*, a collier from South Shields bound for Tromso, was attacked by a German U-boat 25 miles north of Unst. The 25 crew included two Shetlanders and they escaped in the one remaining serviceable lifeboat when the *Sea Venture* was finally torpedoed. The lifeboat made it to Skaw, all the men were saved and the boat has been there ever since.

A salmon hatchery has been established on the Burn of Skaw. The valley has many ruined crofts and with peat available from Saxa Vord, fertile land nearby and fishing, it must have been an attractive place to live.

Lamba Ness will take over an hour to go round and it is a peninsular worth exploring. From the banks overlooking Cudda Stack on its outer-most extremity one can usually view considerable bird activity. The rocks round here are also unforgiving and in February 1936 it was where the Leith trawler, *May Island*, was tragically lost with all hands.

Excavations of pre-Norse houses at Skaw 1972.

38

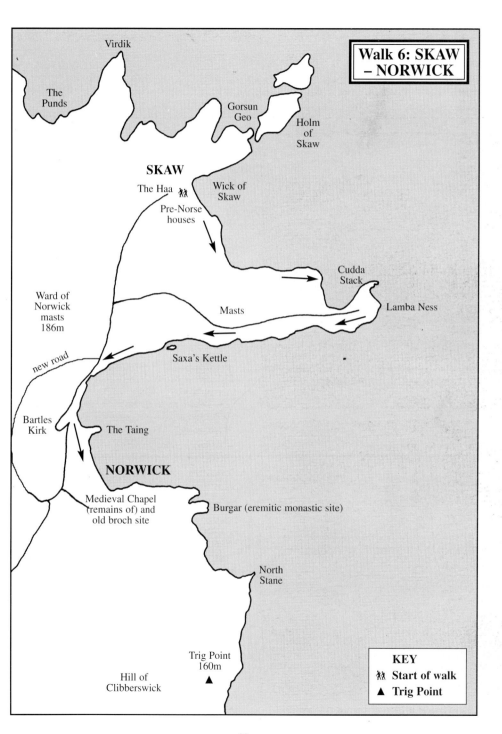

Virdik

The
Punds

Gorsun
Geo

Holm
of
Skaw

SKAW

The Haa 🏃🏃

Wick of
Skaw

Pre-Norse
houses

Cudda
Stack

Lamba Ness

Ward of
Norwick
masts
186m

Masts

new road

Saxa's Kettle

Bartles
Kirk

The Taing

NORWICK

Medieval Chapel
(remains of) and
old broch site

Burgar (eremitic monastic site)

North
Stane

Trig Point
160m
▲

Hill of
Clibberswick

**Walk 6: SKAW
– NORWICK**

KEY

🏃🏃 **Start of walk**

▲ **Trig Point**

Pre-Norse houses and Britain's most northerly beach, Wick of Skaw.

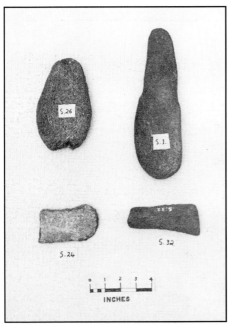

Excavations at Skaw. Iron-Age implements?

The modern masts on Lamba Ness are communication links with the oil fields in the East Shetland Basin. The old ruins date back to World War II when RAF Skaw was an important signals unit. The ruins provide good shelter for the sheep.

Along the southern cliff of Lamba Ness Saxa's Kettle can be viewed. This is an unusual stack, close to the cliff side which has a tunnel at its base through which the sea flows into a circular rock-basin and during a gale it comes to a boil.

It was in the rockbasin that the giant Saxa used to prepare his food. The rival giant Herman sought use of the kettle in which to prepare a whale casserole but was so annoyed when Saxa asked for one half of the whale as a fee that he threw a rock at him from across Burrafirth. Herman's Helyak, or Stack, off Saxa Vord marks the spot where his missile fell.

In reply, Saxa threw a similar sized boulder which landed in the sea off Hermaness and is known as Saxa's Baa.

Hopefully, all you will find flying over Lamba Ness are birds. It is a particularly active place during periods of migration.

Leave Lamba Ness to join the tarmac road the old cliff side part of which is closed to all traffic and takes a steep descent into Nor Wick Bay. Houses at the bottom enjoy extensive views of this lovely bay into which the Burn of Norwick flows, contributing to a wetland area which attracts various wading birds and was once a haaf fishing station. On the beach an outcrop known as The Taing is a main feature. Ray Mitchell excavated four sites here in 1972 and found some pottery and a bone needle which he thought possibly dated from the broch period. In the sandy dunes sea rocket grows and the one kilometre square at Norwick is considered to have one of the greatest variety of breeding birds in all Shetland. In 1695 a French privateer kidnapped, briefly, Miss Craig, the daughter of the Rev. Alexander Craig, minister of Unst from the bay of Norwick. John Tudor actually gives two dates for this incident 1688 and 1695. Now either the Rev Craig had two daughters, both of whom were kidnapped over the years or one daughter who was kidnapped twice. In either case she (or both of them) and the Frenchmen have a lot of explaining to do. Norwick is an active community and celebrates old style Christmas and New Year as well as an Up-Helly-A' night.

At Kirkaton is a burial ground by the war memorial. There can be seen the grass-covered foundation stones of the medieval chapel dedicated to St. John. The 'Inventory' notes that the north wall is slightly curved possibly because it is overlying the foundations of a broch. In the burial ground there are ancient memorials in the shape of rude crosses, some with an incised cross on them. The only remains of the church of St. Bartholomew at Bartles are some boulders, beside which a lamp and stone implements were once found.

The upturned boat which can be seen at the boat house at Kirkaton came from the *Swainby* which was torpedoed by the submarine U13 twenty five miles north of Unst on 17th April, 1940. All 38 crew reached Unst safely so this boat as well as that at Skaw served the crews in the best possible way.

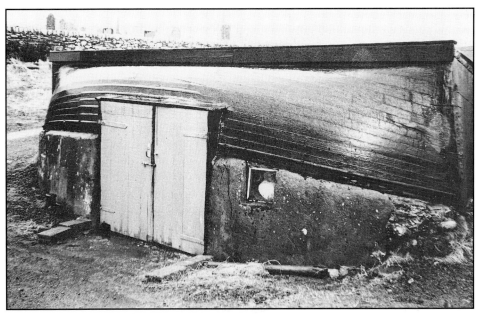

Boat house, Kirkaton, Norwick.

Norwick Beach.

Northern Lights over Norwick. Painting by Liam O'Neill. With kind permission of Gordon and Marjorie Williamson.

WALK 7: NORWICK – HAROLDSWICK

4 miles (6½ kms) : 2 hours

OS Maps: Landranger Sheet 1 Shetland – Yell & Unst
Pathfinder Sheet HP 51/61 Haroldswick

The cliffs at Clibberswick are not too challenging and include a trig point (160m), The Giant and such sexist features as His Geo and Girls Wick. Perhaps the monks on Burgar felt threatened. A great walk with the comforts of Haroldswick awaiting one.

To leave Norwick beach one has to leap over a burn as it reaches the sea on the southern shore and aim along the coastline in the direction of a huge rock which resembles a bear's head. The remains of two water mills will be seen as one crosses the stony but usually sheltered slope which abounds in planticrus.

On Burgar Stack Noel Fojut has identified an eremitic monastic site having spotted traces of house foundations. He warns against using the dangerous rock ridge which links the stack to the shore.

From Burgar one is climbing the Hill of Clibberswick in earnest and when the Horns of Hagmark are reached, where a wire fence warns one not to venture too near the precipitous drop, one has climbed over 400ft (160m). The trig point is very near the drop and if to be touched in windy weather then I suggest an approach is made on hands and knees.

Two cairns were originally recorded on Clibberswick. The one nearest to the trig point was described as being a circular grass covered mound 22ft in diameter and 3ft 6ins high. The other stood on the summit named The Giant but evidently the stones of this cairn were used in the construction of the small roofless building which can be found there now. This was built as a look-out in World War I and is a most desolate construction today. The view of Hamar, Balta and other points south is, however, magnificent.

A descent to view The Nev and go round Rurra

Geo will bring one through an area of over a dozen planticrus. Cross Geo, a rocky beach, is worth exploring and superb samples of serpentine may be found. Talc, which is associated with serpentine, is being quarried commercially and you will have to go round the entrance to the quarry to view the remains of the Cross Kirk. The church, Holy Rude, stands within an

Ancient memorials, Kirkaton, Norwick.

43

enclosure about 50 yards inland from the head of the Cross Geo and extensive remains of its walls survive. Evidently it was for long a place of pilgrimage to which women went to pray for their men at sea.

In 1983 Simon Buttler of the University of Liverpool led a party of archaeologists on an excavation here. His interest was steatite, a talc carbonate rock which has been an important raw material in the history of Shetland, being used for the manufacture of cooking and storage pots, loom weights and other domestic articles.

The cliffs of Cross Ness between North and South Geos show that steatite (soap stone) has been quarried at Clibberswick in the past. There was a Norse period steatite quarry. But Simon Buttler also discovered an Iron Age midden containing bone and pottery fragments, at the landward end of Cross Ness. The puzzle was that there were no obvious signs of ancient settlement.

Another puzzle were the foundations found 200m north of Cross Kirk – local legend says an earlier chapel stood here but there is no written

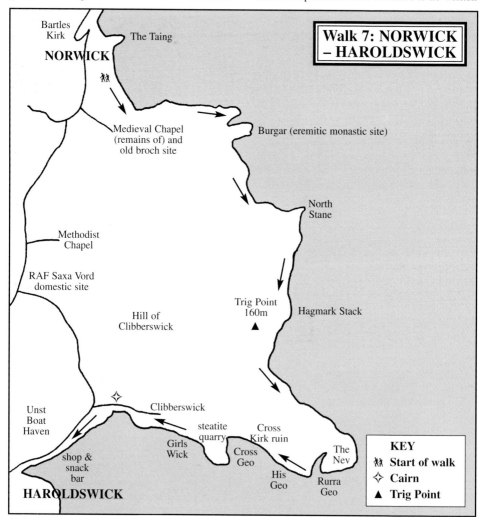

Bartles Kirk

The Taing

NORWICK

Walk 7: NORWICK – HAROLDSWICK

Medieval Chapel (remains of) and old broch site

Burgar (eremitic monastic site)

North Stane

Methodist Chapel

RAF Saxa Vord domestic site

Hill of Clibberswick

Trig Point 160m
▲

Hagmark Stack

Unst Boat Haven

Clibberswick

steatite quarry

Cross Kirk ruin

shop & snack bar

Girls Wick

Cross Geo

The Nev

His Geo

Rurra Geo

HAROLDSWICK

KEY

𝄍 **Start of walk**

✧ **Cairn**

▲ **Trig Point**

Andrew Priest of Norwick sets out tea.

Sea Rocket, Norwick.

The pottery in the midden was consistent with Wheelhouse Period domestic sites elsewhere in Shetland, for example the houses near the edge of the cliffs at Skaw. The conclusion is that an iron age settlement with wheelhouses stood at the edge of the cliffs here which have since been removed by natural erosion, Norse quarrying and the effect of a mine exploding on the cliff in World War II.

The houses at Clibberswick can be reached by a track and from there a road goes to Haroldswick. Alternatively, it is rather a scramble along the foreshore where there seem to be more than the usual number of springs, wire fences and walls which shelter the Shetland ponies. Some magnificent domed stone cairns by the North Booth welcome one into Haroldswick.

Trevor Hunter plays a traditional Shetland fiddle tune for Magnie Sinclair to broadcast over the CB.

evidence of this. Jessie Saxby, in an article 'Sacred Sites in a Shetland Isle' (1905) re-ported, "there is a circular steede' (foundations of the supposed old kirks of Unst) near the brow of the cliff at Cruigeo".

Haroldswick is a tourist centre and has a shop serving snacks. Nearby are Nikka Vord and Crussa Field which have a wealth of cairns and stone circles. A medieval chapel site at Bothen, dedicated to St. Mary can be found between Bothen and the former Haroldswick Primary

Unst Boat Haven, Haroldswick. Mural by Liam O'Neill.

School now the new Heritage Centre, with walls within a burial ground enclosure. The walls have been built with very large stones. The 'Inventory' noted outside the east gable a badly weathered decorated tombstone commemorating the Mowat and Bruce family. High in the hills above the village, the White Haggle (125m) and the White Stane of Housifield (100m) are prominent.

Allow time to visit the Unst Boat Haven behind Skibhoul Stores which has a superb collection of Shetland traditional boats with a backdrop painted by local artist Liam O'Neill. The Unst Heritage Centre also has permanent displays and exhibitions showing various aspects of the history of Unst and the people who live there as well as extensive genealogy records.

The road to Norwick takes one past the domestic site of RAF Saxa Vord with its modern accommodation buildings. The station crest includes a Viking longship.

RAF Saxa Vord station crest.

Happy memories come crowding back to me when I view the site, particularly of the Unst people who worked at RAF Saxa Vord. Hughie McMeechan was the first person I got to know well – just the sort of person to meet on arrival at a new location – and, because I lived near the incinerator building, I soon met the cleaning team known as 'The White Tornados', Lew, Big John and Tap Tap. A concoction was once given to me by them to sample and when I hesitated to drink it I was reassured with the comforting news that, "it burned with a blue flame": Of Sgt Frank Brand who lead the first servicemen to arrive at the base in October 1956. He was in effect the first commanding officer. In retirement as a civilian steward in the Officer's Mess he was asked to find out how many guests, which included VIPs from London, would like soup to start their special luncheon. He went into the ante-room where drinks were being served, cleared his throat and shouted out to a somewhat startled throng, "hands up those who want soup." And where would Wing Commander Ron Sparkes have been without Bertie the Butcher? Before the advent of the inter-island car ferries the cash to pay both civilians and servicemen would arrive

Hughie McMeechan on clappers and Frances Hunter on bass, of the Uyeasound Band.

on the *Earl of Zetland* from Lerwick on a Thursday. However gales could delay its arrival in which case Bertie would give Saxa Vord a considerable sum in cash to tide it over until the boat came in. A unique arrangement.

Between RAF Saxa Vord and Norwick pass a ruined Methodist chapel on the left and a little further up, on the right, the access road to the new Methodist Chapel where services are held most Sundays. The first chapel was built in 1829, it was enlarged in 1856 and then replaced by a second chapel in 1881. Other Methodist preaching places in Unst included Colvadale, Underhoull, Skaw, Norwick, Haroldswick, Muness, Clibberswick, Baliasta, Houlland, and on Uyea Isle. Between 1928-1931 the Rev. Bertram Woods was serving his probationary period here and was inspired to compose a

lovely tune to the hymn "O Jesus I have Promised". He named the tune "Norwick". In 1990 I bought a holiday cottage in Daniel Place, Penzance and discovered it was the same street in which Rev. Woods had lived out his retirement. He had spent much of his ministry in East Anglia and Mrs. Woods told me that many people thought that the hymn's name Norwick was a misspelling of Norwich! It was the 'First Tune' in the 1933 edition of the Methodist Hymn Book. As the congregation assembled for the dedication service of Britain's new northernmost church in May 1993 it was 'Norwick' which was fittingly being played on the organ – a reminder of the sources of inspiration which both the area and its chapel have been to people over many, many years. It therefore seems appropriate to include it in this guide (below).

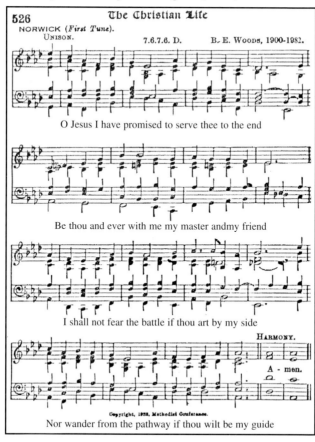

526   The Christian Life

NORWICK (*First Tune*).
UNISON.   7.6.7.6. D.   B. E. WOODS, 1900-1982.

O Jesus I have promised to serve thee to the end

Be thou and ever with me my master andmy friend

I shall not fear the battle if thou art by my side

HARMONY.

A - men.

Copyright, 1933, Methodist Conference.
Nor wander from the pathway if thou wilt be my guide

WALK 8: HAROLDSWICK – BALTASOUND

4½ miles (7½ kms) : 2 hours

OS Maps: **Landranger Sheet 1 Shetland – Yell & Unst**
Pathfinder Sheet HP 40/50/60 Baltasound
HP 51/61 Haroldswick

Note: Scottish Natural Heritage (SNH) has published an information leaflet on the National Nature Reserve on the Keen of Hamar, (Tel: 01595 693345).

The diversity of Unst is appreciated on this walk which is dominated by visiting the National Nature Reserve on the Keen of Hamar, 19th century chromite quarries and a variety of interesting features that help to make Baltasound so attractive.

Leave Haroldswick by the main road, the

wetland area near the junction with the road to Burra Firth may have waders or geese on it. Leave the road after a slipway as it begins to ascend Setters Hill by climbing left over the wall. The walk round Soterberg is rocky and marshy and below Setters quarry is a stone wall and ruin.

Continue round the coastline into the Wick of Hagdale by following the remains of an ancient stone wall to its south. The croft of Hagdale and the ruin of a circular stone built 'Horse Mill', complete with mill stones, lie between the Geo

Walk 8: HAROLDSWICK – BALTASOUND

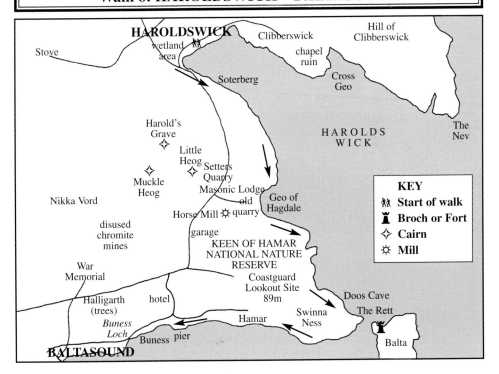

of Hagdale and the main road. The horse-powered mill crushed the heavy iron chromate which then remained in the central reservoir until the impurities were flushed away by water. Chromite from the 19th century iron chromate quarried in the Hagdale area was used for explosives and for metal plating. Serpentine was also quarried near here. The building nearer the road is Masonic Lodge Aurora No. 1654.

Cross the burn and commence the ascent of Hamar by crossing over a wire fence and aiming for the peak of the hill. The top is devoid of pasture and has been described as, "a unique area of serpentine supporting a number of arctic alpine plants and exhibiting active periglaciar features at the lowest altitude to be found in the British Isles". Do not pick any flowers or damage plant life. The landscape is believed to resemble that which covered much of Britain at the end of the last ice age.

It was this area perhaps that the famous botanist Thomas Edmonston (1825 – 1845) at the age of 12 discovered the two plants, Arenaria Norvegic (Norwegian Sandwort) and Cerasrum

Nigrescens (Alpine Chickweed) which have since been associated with his name. Scottish Sandwort, Shepherd's Cress, Hairy Whitlow Grass, Frog Orchid and Stone Bramble may be found here. Leave the reserve by crossing a stile in front of a dilapidated Coastguard Lookout and descend the slope past Ramnaberg and on to Swinna Ness. Across the turbulent waters of the Rett is the island of Balta and from a wall and stone enclosure on the point of the ness it is possible to see the ruined building on the broch site on the North East corner of Balta. Turn into Balta Sound past a ruined croft house and the rest of the walk is like walking through a well kept park. There are little footbridges and stiles and beyond Hamar a small tarn which hosts an occasional duck. Note the remains of piers associated with the herring stations. Hamar was the home of Charles Sandison and his book "Unst – My Island Home and Its Story" (The Shetland Times 1968) is essential reading for those who wish to enjoy a very personal account of the history of Unst. Salmon cages are now sited in the sound and after reaching a cattle grid leave the coast to follow the road

Buness, the Boit and Kater Stones in foreground.

round Alex Sandison and Son Ltd., quarry-masters, hauliers and now salmon hatchery operators amongst other things. Opposite the works entrance was a building which until the 1950s and complete with bell tower was the 'Swedish Church'. Built in 1910, the church met the needs of Scandinavian fishermen during the spring and summer. A Swedish pastor used to come for several weeks each year. Sadly the church, then in retirement as a boat store, blew down in the great gale of 1991 and Duncan Sandison's replica sixareen was destroyed. There is now a stone commemorating the Swedish church and in 1993 another replica sixareen, the *Far Haaf* was built. The original pier was once a sailing ship but in 1903 she was brought to Baltasound by a tug and anchored in the harbour as a coal hulk. In 1911 she was taken ashore and "placed to form a useful 120ft extension to the existing stage and surrounded by a concrete wall and filled in", wrote Charles Sandison.

Now a modern pier has been constructed to meet the needs of Unst's industrial and crofting activities and a marina for the Unst Boating Club.

The Baltasound Hotel is north, a few yards straight up the road behind the pier.

Follow the coastal road passing stone noosts and a small pier until Buness is reached. This is the ancestral home of the Edmonston family and it has seen many important visitors. In 1814 the "Wizard of the North", Sir Walter Scott, made a brief visit to Shetland. It is thought Dr. Arthur Edmonston was his guide and gave him the background material for Scott's novel "The Pirate". The artist John Reid was so entranced he returned "to Buness about midnight, I did not go to bed, but rested on the sofa for two hours". On the lawn in front of the main building two stones are visible, one erect on the other with the following inscription recording "Kater's Experiment". –

To this stone were attached the clock and pendulum employed by the celebrated French philosopher Biot and on the one on which it rests stood his repeating

circle. The distinguished English philosopher Kater placed his repeating circle on this stone also.

The former was sent by the Institute of France in the summer of 1817 and the latter by the Royal Society of London in the summer of 1818 to determine by their experiments and observations the figure of the earth.

One of the Kater Stones restored by David Edmonston.

51

These memorials remain as pleasing and lasting remembrances of the splendid talents, great worth and amiable manners of those eminent men by their friend Thomas Edmonston. 21st October 1818

David Edmonston, the present laird, has recently restored the lettering.

From the shoreline Halligarth, once the home of the Saxby family, is visible with its plantation of trees known irreverently as 'Saxby's Forest'. The trees were actually planted by Laurence Edmonston and have attracted a variety of birds including the resident long-eared owls. The Saxby family includes many who have contributed to Shetland literature, particularly famous being Jessie Saxby who, when she was 90 years old, published her final work, "Shetland Traditional Lore" (Grant & Murray 1932). Her description of the Unst giants Saxa and Herman is particularly appealing.

Follow the pebbly foreshore over a burn and past a noost where the boat sits on a wheeled trailer to run down a pair of rails into the sea. There is a good saltmarsh at the head of the sound. Pass a children's' play park to go to the main shop for the area at Skibhoul Stores (meaning, "the hill from which they watch for ships"), licensed general merchants, bakers (and home of Skibhoul's 'Special Biscuits') souvenirs, petrol and diesel. The Post Office, now UK's most northerly, is nearby as is the

Long-eared owl in "Saxby's Forest", Halligarth, Baltasound.

Hillside Free Church, Baltasound. Note carving of the "burning bush" (Exodus, Chapter 3) and date (1843). The burning bush is now the symbol of the Church of Scotland.

Baltasound Community Hall (Unst Working Men's Society).

West along the main road is the imposing Parish Church of St. John which was built in 1827 with a bell tower dated 1959. Opposite is the new care centre and behind that the Henderson General Stores at Nord. Nord, during the herring fishing was the Nord Hotel. Still further west is the doctor's surgery at Hillsgarth (built originally as the Church of Scotland manse) and the junior high school with a plantation and a small tarn. Adjacent to the school is the fine leisure centre providing many facilities, including an excellent indoor heated swimming pool. Beyond the manse is a derelict, roofless United Free Church dated 1843. The 'Hillside' Free Kirk survived the 1929 reconciliation between the Free Church and the Church of Scotland because 160 members voted to 'stay out', but in 1963 it finally became redundant. One minister, the Rev. Ingram, lived to be in charge of both old and new Church of Scotland Churches and at the 'Disruption' became the Free Church minister of Unst. He lived to the age of 102 years and 11 months so it must have been a healthy occupation.

A little further along the road there was once a cairn near the ruined Kirk of Baliasta described as a stone circle 67ft in diameter. There is conjecture that the circles on Crussa Field (Walk H) were a place of trial and that a prisoner if found guilty had a sort of right of appeal as in Tingwall. In Unst he could make a dash for the circle near Baliasta or to the actual church to gain sanctuary and pardon if not struck down en-route. The parts of the medieval church of St. John are visible in the lower part of the north wall of the later, now derelict, church built in 1764. There is a stone stile in the wall of the burial ground. This church was abandoned with the building of the 'Muckle Kirk', the western half of which is now St. John's church Baltasound, in 1827.

By way of contrast Baltasound also boasts Shetland's only brewery, Valhalla, which brews the excellent beers 'Auld Rock' and 'White Wife'.

To the north of Baltasound above the war memorial, gifted by Jessie Saxby in 1932, on the slopes of Nikka Vord and Hagdale are disused chromite mines. They are considered the best sites for studying these ore deposits in Britain. Discovered in 1817 by Hibbert, chromite was quarried until, unable to compete with foreign ores of a higher grade, the last stock of ore was disposed of in 1932. Also on the road to Hagdale is a garage and coach hire business with both petrol and diesel refueling facilities.

WALK 9: BALTASOUND – MUNESS CASTLE

8½ miles (14 kms) : 4 hours

OS Maps: Landranger Sheet 1 Shetland – Yell & Unst
Pathfinder Sheet HP 40/50/60 Baltasound

Easy walking can be enjoyed along this low lying stretch of Unst's east coast which for centuries was a popular place to live. The ruins of the crofting area of Colvadale contrast with those of medieval Framgord Chapel, Pictish and Viking ruins at Sandwick and finally the 17th century castle at Muness. Teas and snacks are available at Nornova Knitwear.

Follow the southern shore of Balta Sound signposted for Ordale. Along the shore are many remains of piers used at the height of the great herring fishing from about 1880 to about 1925. At the height of it, in 1905, it is said one could walk from one side of the sound to the other, so tightly packed were the 700 boats using one of the world's largest herring ports. The temporary population of Unst could reach over 8,000 during the herring season and included many "gutter girls" who were accommodated in huts along the foreshore.

Model of accommodation hut for girls who gutted the fish. Courtesy of Duncan and Janet Sandison.

Springfield Herring Station, Baltasound, 1906 (Sandison's Pier).

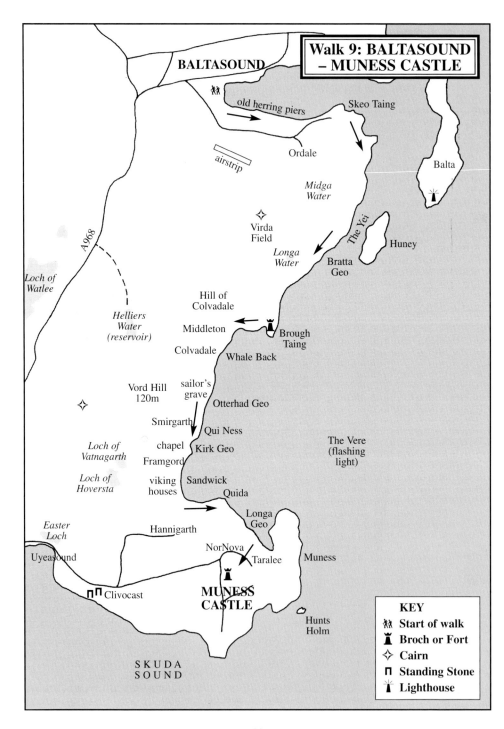

Walk 9: BALTASOUND – MUNESS CASTLE

BALTASOUND

old herring piers

Skeo Taing

airstrip

Ordale

Balta

Midga Water

Virda Field

Longa Water

The Yei

Huney

Bratta Geo

Loch of Watlee

Helliers Water (reservoir)

Hill of Colvadale

Middleton

Colvadale

Whale Back

Brough Taing

A968

Vord Hill 120m

sailor's grave

Otterhad Geo

Smirgarth

Qui Ness

The Vere (flashing light)

Loch of Vatnagarth

chapel

Framgord

Kirk Geo

Loch of Hoversta

viking houses

Sandwick

Quida

Easter Loch

Hannigarth

Longa Geo

Uyeasound

NorNova

Taralee

Muness

Clivocast

MUNESS CASTLE

Hunts Holm

SKUDA SOUND

KEY

🚶 Start of walk
🏰 Broch or Fort
✧ Cairn
⌐ Standing Stone
🗼 Lighthouse

56

Herring boats, Baltasound, in 1900.

Walk past remains of a former factory in the herring era and on towards Skeo Taing (a skeo was an unmortared stone building built on an exposed site through which air could pass to dry meat and fish hanging within) and one begins to appreciate again the length and height of Balta Island and how much protection it gives to Balta Sound Harbour.

Turn south and the first of many well built stone walls is encountered. A flashing strobe light indicates a communications mast set in an enclosure but this does not appear to affect the otters which may be seen near the ruined croft at The Yei. Here are the narrows separating Unst from the island of Huney and the clear blue water and sandy bottom of The Yei may tempt one to cross this ayre at low water.

Off the east coast of Huney, over 100ft below the surface of the sea, lies the wreck of the Royal Navy submarine 'E49'. Launched in 1916 it measured 181ft long and displaced 800 tons. On 10th March 1917 'E49' was on patrol off Muckle Flugga in high seas and on the morning of the 11th the submarine put into

Swedish Fishermens Memorial, Baltasound

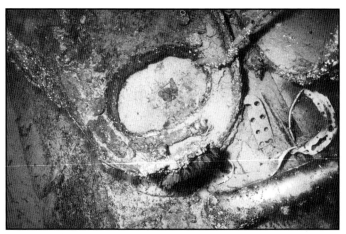

Submarine E49 conning tower and hatch.

Baltasound to carry out repairs. On the morning of the 12th the 'E49' left on her last voyage, for at 1300 hours, shortly after she left the south entrance, an explosion was heard. The 'E49' sank with all hands having struck a mine laid by a German submarine. A diver went down to the wreck on 15th March and reported a hole 6ft by 8ft in her starboard bow; the wreck was left in position and declared an official war grave.

On 4th August 1988 the wreck was again rediscovered by members of the Shetland Sub-Aqua Club and in accordance with the requirements stated in a letter from the Ministry of Defence the divers did not enter or disturb the submarine at all. Andy Carter, one of the members of the team, later wrote, "We left E49 just as we'd found her. Nothing was touched or broken off. Seventy one years ago a group of young men, probably much like ourselves, had gone down with that boat. We left E49 to rest in peace".

After Bratta Geo the foreshore becomes extremely craggy and a search for the broch at Brough Taing is disappointing. Evidently a severe gale in February 1900 left the area strewn with debris so there is no structural evidence of a broch ever having been here. Not much either of St. John's Church at Colvadale, a deserted crofting area with over a dozen ruined crofts, planticrus and four noosts. I have

yet to find a whale at Whale Back but stranded whales are not uncommon in Unst. A German sailor's grave is marked by a stake at the head of the grave. It is approximately 180yds north of the Hilldyke separating Colvadale from Smirgarth and about 10yds from the edge of the low cliff. It could date from the 1st World War or even earlier. The hills above Colvadale have cairns as guides for both onshore and offshore navigation. There is an "escape route" to the main road via Unst's main reservoir at Helliers Water and it is from that direction that the Burn of Vatsdeild descends.

Cross the burn by derelict stone bridge. There are many stone ruins including a curious L-shaped wall with stony mound inside. The terrain becomes marshy and stone clearance cairns abound – relics of the era of cultivation. A wooden stile helps one through another stone wall and so past Otterhad Geo and Qui Ness to the area of Sandwick. At Framgord is an ancient chapel, dedicated to St. Mary, sometimes referred to as Eastings, within the burial ground for the area, (access either by gate or by unusual stone stile on western wall of enclosure). It is rectangular in shape measuring 40ft by 12ft. Inside the chapel there is a late seventeenth century memorial stone, so weathered that only the letters AB, beside the cartouche on which the coat of arms was represented, can be deciphered. The burial ground is very interesting as it contains both ancient upright stones with crosses and recumbent slabs with either a cross or a central rib on the upper surfaces.

Sandwick has one of Unst's loveliest white sandy beaches and under the scrutiny of a massive boulder in the hill above, cross the beach towards large ruined stone buildings and enclosure. The conclusions of the archaeological research carried out in 1977 and 1978 were that the buildings date back to the late Norse period (1100 – 1500 AD). Keep a watch out because relics of various kinds are frequently picked up close to high water mark around Sandwick Bay! The sand covered hillocks have from time to time been partially devastated, exposing large stones in the interior which have been given the name "The Vikings' Graves". It has not been possible to confirm that a broch existed in the bay but relics collected include shards resembling broch pottery, whorls, combs and pins so there probably was one. A display of artefacts found at Sandwick can be seen in the Shetland Museum.

Cross a stile to the southern shore and the landscape changes as progress is made round the area of Muness where there is a tourist centre in the knitwear and crafts shop at NorNova (snacks and teas).

Small geos indent the coastline, the land has been reseeded and at the Ham of Muness is a sheltered bay. From a pebbly beach at Tarlee are visible the houses and castle of Muness and a track leads up to them. The castle (key available from the croft opposite) a typical feudal residence of the 16th century, consists of an oblong building with round towers at the NE and SW, angles and hanging turrets at the other corner. The windows show much variety in design, there are gun loops in the walls and the ground floor is vaulted.

On a panel above the doorway in the south wall is the following inscription in late Gothic lettering:

LIST ZE TO KNAW YIS BULDING QUHA BEGAN LAURENCE THE BRUCE HE WAS THAT WORTHY MAN QUHA ERNESTLY HIS AIRIS AND OFSPRING PRAY IS TO HELP AND NOT TO HURT THIS VARK ALUAYIS followed by THE ZEIR OF GOD 1598 in Roman lettering.

An armorial panel higher up bears the Bruce arms flanked with the initials L.B. for Laurence Bruce.

The castle remained inhabited until 1699 when the last direct heir, Andrew Bruce, drowned.

Muness Castle (south wall).

WALK 10: MUNESS – UYEASOUND

5 miles (8 kms) : 2 hours

OS Maps: Landranger Sheet 1 Shetland – Yell & Unst
                Pathfinder Sheet HP 40/50/60 Baltasound
                HU 59/69 Fetlar (north)

A walk offering the delightfully scenic sea views to be enjoyed round Muness contrasting with the enclosed waters of Skuda Sound. Two standing stones, the one at Clivocast being particularly striking, can be sought out as can the ruins of the 'disappearing church', Gletna Kirk, on reaching the lovely haven of Uyeasound.

Return to the coastline at Taralee and continue round Ham Ness, passing distinctive Breiwick and the Stack of Kideo before walking above Holm Sound and dropping down to Scolla Wick. To the south, between Unst and Fetlar, the National Nature Reserve island of Haaf Gruney can be seen, "Grunie yields serpentine of a superior quality, which takes on a high polish, and might be useful for ornamental stonework", wrote Dr. Cowie in 1879. Many people treasure model croft houses and clocks made of local serpentine by the late Tom Hughson. Some of the lintels in the Lerwick Town Hall came from Haaf Gruney. At the Ness

of Ramnageo one is opposite the high East Neap and Vord Hill of Fetlar – an island which stays visible until Uyea Island blocks the view. From Ore Wick one can ascend north to view two standing stones.

Nearest the shore, near the NE corner of the park to the east of the barns on the SE side of Clivocast, is a standing stone of pyramidal shape 3ft 2in high. Base girth is 6ft 4in. About 60ft south a barely discernible mound, a possible Viking grave, was excavated in 1875 to reveal human remains and armour.

Climb up through the fields slightly northeast to find, alongside the road on its south side between Clivocast and Muness, a prominent

Tom Hughson of Uyeasound with an American friend holding one of his serpentine models of a crofthouse.

Standing stone, Clivocast, Uyeasound.

monolith of schist leaning a little towards the NE on a deviation of 100ft above the sea. It rises to a height of 9ft 10in (3 metres) and at the base is 2ft 10in wide (0.9 metres) by 1ft ½in thick the broader sides facing almost north and south.

Back on the coastline the lighthouse on the western shore of Uyea Sound comes into view though the village itself is out of sight until the Cliva Skerries are passed.

Join the road at the housing estate near an old jetty and walk east noting the distinctive Up-Helly-A' galley shed. Pass in front of the school and the classically attractive Church of Scotland church which is situated opposite it. Along the foreshore we come to Easter Loch on the right hand side. This loch is particularly noted for the activity during the winter months

Standing stone south east of Clivocast (arrow points to standing stone of Clivocast).

Walk 10: MUNESS CASTLE– UYEASOUND

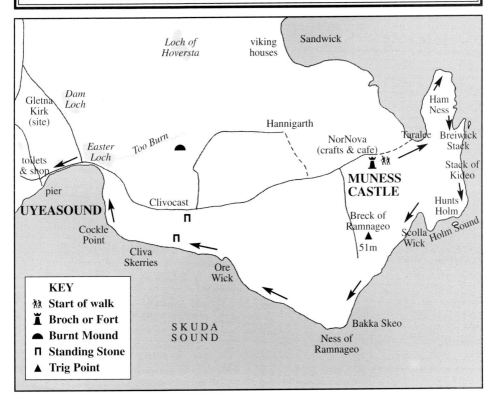

Easter Loch, Uyeasound, and Whooper Swans.

when many ducks and sometimes over 100 whooper swans winter here. The swans are thought to come mainly from Iceland and come south to the same wintering sites each year. The adult swans are all white but with a distinguishing feature in that the bill is yellow at the base (the mute swan has an orange tip to its bill). The whooper also has a distinctive voice which is a loud clanging 'ah ng'ha' noise. Easter Loch is shallow, has plenty of dead vegetation and is near the sea which makes it such a favourite for the swans.

In 1911 the first Unst Up-Helly-A' was cele-brated here and the Uyeasound Up-Helly-A' guizers follow the Jarl's squad and the Viking galley from the shed and along the foreshore to the burning area each February. It is a magni-ficent sight to see the flames of the torches reflected in the loch and waves of the sea. The guizers perform their acts in the Uyeasound Community Hall (South Unst Peoples' Insti-tute).

To the loch's north east is Too Burn beside which is one of Unst's burnt mounds.

The road going north of the loch's western shore takes one past Dam Loch (occasional whooper swans) opposite the remains of Gletna Kirk. Legend tells that this was the "unfinished

kirk". Because the church was being built on the site of an ancient dwelling the 'powers of darkness' removed at night whatever had been built during the day – certainly only rough foundations remain on the west side of the road and measure 61ft 5in from E to W by 24ft 5in from N to S. The National Museum possesses a collection of fragments of unglazed pottery from this ruin which suggests the church may have become a domestic house at some time.

Back on the sea shore we pass Scata Water (Wester Loch) which is also popular with ducks. The main jetty at Uyeasound is round the bay and has become a busy place with salmon farm activity. It has seen busier days for Uyeasound was once an important port for trade with Leith and herring stations were established here in the opening years of the last century. Up from the pier is the partly restored Greenwell Booth, used in the Hanseatic trading days. Relief may be obtained at the public toilets adjacent to the booth, in a building which blends well with others near it.

The Westside shop faces the pier and the Gardiesfauld Hostel, a very handy place for accommodation, is just round the corner. Opposite the hostel is Musselburgh which tradition tells is built on the site of the broch which once dominated the bay of Uyea Sound.

62

WALK 11: UYEASOUND – BELMONT █████████

3 miles (5 kms) : 2 hours

OS Maps: **Landranger Sheet 1 Shetland – Yell & Unst**
Pathfinder Sheet HP 40/50/60 Baltasound
HU 59/69 Fetlar (north)

If you started at Belmont then this is the final stretch of your Round Unst Trek. It is easy walking and one leaves the beauty and shelter of Uyeasound to round a headland which contains interesting prehistoric sites and good otter watching possibilities.

From the jetty in Uyeasound walk south-west to follow the coastline past the lighthouse, the remains of an old pier and the site of a grave of a drowned mariner, to round the point of Burk Well. This grave is defined by an outline of stones but its date has not been established. The Holm of Heogland comes into view, access to this small tidal island is possible at low water.

Between the loch of Heogland and Belmont there are usually signs of otter activity. At Head

of Mula in the middle of the land of the abandoned croft is a late iron age oval house site which has produced pottery of the wheel house type.

If time allows it is worth climbing 250ft up the south slope of Gallow Hill to a heel-shaped cairn, 4ft high with the interior and the façade considerably masked by tumbled stones but with the kerb well defined. Within the cairn are traces of a circular kerb. Three large stones are apparently part of a passage leading to a chamber defined by three slabs set on edge.

Continue along the banks to see Belmont come into view and on reaching the ferry terminal you complete the Round Unst Trek.

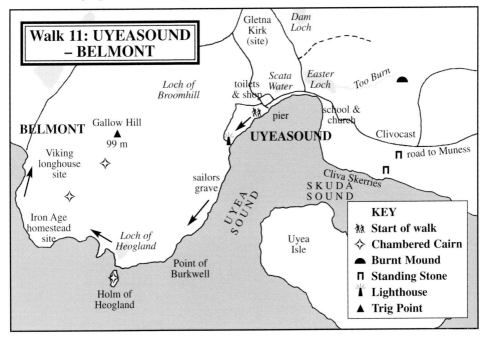

Walk 11: UYEASOUND – BELMONT

Gletna Kirk (site)

Dam Loch

Loch of Broomhill

Scata Water

Easter Loch

Too Burn

toilets & shop

pier

school & church

BELMONT

Gallow Hill
▲
99 m

Viking longhouse site ✧

✧

UYEASOUND

Clivocast

⊓ road to Muness

sailors grave

⊓

Iron Age homestead site

Loch of Heogland

UYEA SOUND

Cliva Skerries
SKUDA
SOUND

Uyea Isle

Point of Burkwell

Holm of Heogland

KEY
🏃 **Start of walk**
✧ **Chambered Cairn**
⬤ **Burnt Mound**
⊓ **Standing Stone**
⊺ **Lighthouse**
▲ **Trig Point**

CIRCULAR WALK A

BELMONT – SNABROUGH

3½ miles (7½ kms) : 2½ hours

OS Maps: Landranger Sheet 1 Shetland – Yell & Unst
                 Pathfinder Sheet HP 40/50/60 Baltasound

Not only is the coastline of Unst towards Blue Mull enjoyed on this walk but also that of North Yell. A heritage walk, it includes two brochs, a deserted crofting area and an 18th century mansion.

From Belmont Ferry Terminal (toilets) take the road north leaving it to go down to the beach and walk round the Wick of Belmont. The path along the cliff edge is very narrow so you may prefer to stay on the beach. At Hoga Ness is the ruin of a broch and it is worth exploring the massive ramparts and ditches before heading north to Snarra Voe, where the Yell ferry used to cross from. Brei Geo, opposite Ness of Cullivoe on Yell, is a popular nesting area for fulmars. Turn inland directly east to reach the northern shore of Loch of Snabrough – one of my

---

Cicrular Walk A: BELMONT – SNABROUGH

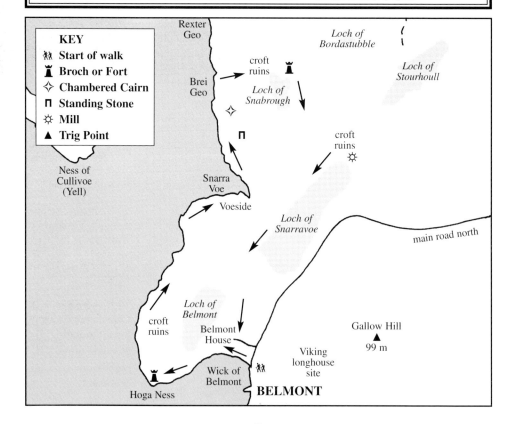

KEY

🏃 Start of walk
🏛 Broch or Fort
✧ Chambered Cairn
⊓ Standing Stone
☼ Mill
▲ Trig Point

Rexter Geo

Loch of Bordastubble

croft ruins

Loch of Stourhoull

Brei Geo

Loch of Snabrough

croft ruins
☼

Ness of Cullivoe (Yell)

Snarra Voe

Voeside

Loch of Snarravoe

main road north

croft ruins

Loch of Belmont

Belmont House

Gallow Hill
▲
99 m

Viking longhouse site

Wick of Belmont

Hoga Ness

BELMONT

Standing stone, Snarravoe.

favourite spots in Shetland. The ruined croft houses of Easterhouse, Westerhouse and Sotherhouse are presumably built from the stone of the broch on the northern shore, now in a very ruinous condition. It has been estimated that the overall diameter was about 60ft and internal diameter about 27ft. On the south side the loch provided protection but on the landward side there was a strong wall and ditch which curved across the broad neck of the promontory. In summer one can sit and enjoy the view from the broch which can include otter and red-throated diver; in winter the loch is visited by duck.

Just beyond the south shore of the loch are some ancient cairns and a prehistoric homestead site and directly south of them the deserted crofting settlement of Snarravoe, with its small lynchetted fields much in evidence. At the north end of Loch of Snarravoe is a ruined water mill with part of the mill stone once driven by the burn flowing down from Loch of Stourhoull.

From the evocative ruins of the Snarravoe crofts walk down the eastern shore to cross a footbridge in a marshy area and make for Belmont House. This splendid mansion, built in 1775, is in the process of being restored having been virtually uninhabited since 1914.

Take a track from the E of the house to walk down to the road and return to the Belmont ferry terminal.

CIRCULAR WALK B

BORDASTUBBLE STANDING STONE – LUNDA WICK
3 miles (5 kms) : 2½ hours

OS Maps: Landranger Sheet 1 Shetland – Yell & Unst
Pathfinder Sheet HP 40/50/60 Baltasound

There is a lot to see on this walk: a haunted ruined mansion, medieval church, a broch, viking settlement and four standing stones. All in three miles!

From the A968 take the road to Westing; ½ mile (1 km) along this road take the left turn to Lund and the standing stone of Bordastubble will shortly hove into view after crossing delightful Burn of Vinstrick.

The magnificent standing stone of Bordastubble stands just off the road and is reputed to be "Shetland's most massive". It is about 12ft

(3.8m) high with its major axis NW and SE. Four feet above the ground its girth is 22ft and its width 8ft 2ins (2.7m). It shows a definite lean to the SW and the packing stones at its base may have been placed to stop the mighty monolith from leaning any further.

There is now an option to leave the road at a cattle grid near this stone and climb the hill beside a wire fence and remains of a stone wall. At the top of the hill, east of the Loch of Bordastubble where two fences meet, is a dilapidated cairn of stones and a standing stone. It is roughly triangular about 4ft high with slight

Circular Walk B: BORDASTUBBLE STANDING STONE – LUNDA WICK

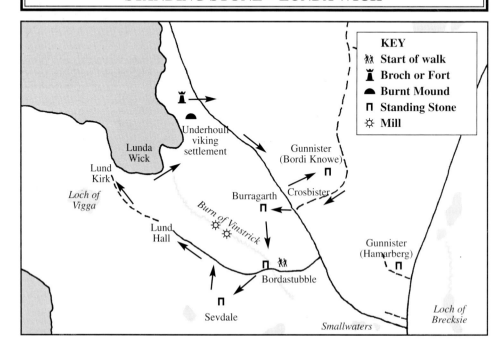

inclination to the west. Locally it is known as the standing stone of Sevdale. Walk back down the hill to walk the road to Lund where the unsafe ruin of Lund Hall can be seen. The hall was built in the early 18th century but the roof was removed in 1947 and it is deteriorating fast. It has probably never recovered from a visit by the Devil – and he didn't dally, just stayed long enough to leave an imprint of a hoof on one of the flagstones. The ruined Hall looks down on the ruined, also roofless, 12th century church of St Olaf. Here can be seen many interesting head stones including two tombs of Bremen merchants and others described in Walk 1.

Walk round the bay and at the E shore climb to explore the ruins of the early 9th century Norse houses which includes a boat shaped Norse longhouse which has been constructed from earlier Iron Age round houses on the same site. Above the Norse farmstead is the broch of Underhoull on the top of a prominent knoll near the road. Although the walls have practically disappeared two ramparts with a wide intervening ditch are visible.

Now take the road in the SE direction until the sign to Burragarth is reached on the right. There

Standing Stone of Bordastubble (Lund Haa in the background).

Lund Haa.

Taking the strain (i). The Standing Stone of Sevdale.

Taking the strain (ii). The Standing Stone of Burragarth.

Sculptured Stone of Hamarberg, Gunnister. "Like a Cornish pasty!"

The Standing Stone of Gunnister.

are three crofts in the area and at the top of the knoll behind the crofts, again acting as a straining post where two fences meet, is the standing stone of Burragarth. It is not easy to see until near it as it only rises to a height of 3ft with a girth of 7ft at its base. From this stone head south to cross the Burn of Vinstrick which flows fast down to the sea past the ruins of two watermills and so return to the stone of Bordastubble, unless you want to track down a final standing stone.

From the stone of Burragarth, roughly ½ mile in a NE direction is the Stone of Gunnister (Bordi Knowe) to avoid confusion with Gunnister (Hamarberg). On the left of the road above Crosbister is a hillroad and on a plateau, with excellent views of Lunda Wick and the ruined kirk, the stone will be found. Its height is 2ft 6ins, width is nearly 3ft and thickness about 1ft. The 'Inventory' thinks it may have been higher and it noted a 4ft portion of stone to the NW deeply embedded in the turf which could have been broken off what is left.

There is one other stone of interest in the area. Just north of the junction between the Westings road and the main Belmont – Baltasound road a track goes up to the busy croft of Gunnister (Hamarberg). Follow the track, over a cattle grid until a gate is reached. To the right of the gate is a stile and just to the right after you have climbed the stile is the sculptured stone of Hamarberg. With its series of man-made depressions on its roughly oval shape 6ft 4ins by 3ft 3ins it has a remarkable resemblance to a Cornish Pasty. Presumably these 'cup marks' were of some significance. Irvine's 'miscellanea' states that, "on a bare summit of the rock over its site was held the earliest Law Ting Court in Shetland, afterwards removed to Tingwall". Were they trying to move the stone down to Tingwall and gave up the idea at this point?

"What were you?". Standing stones, Gunnister.

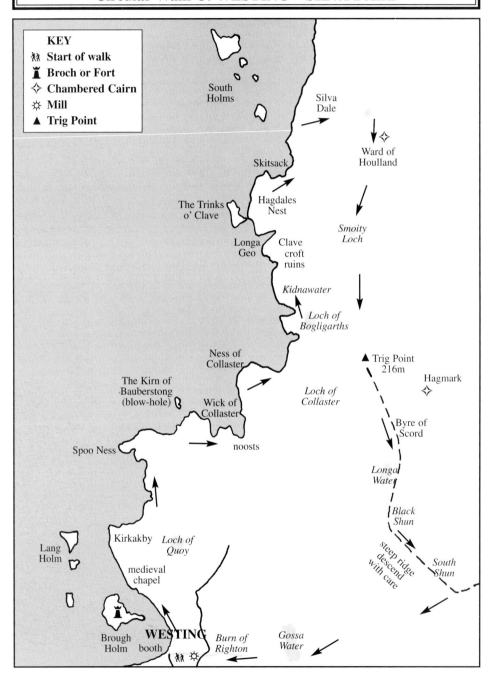

KEY
- 𝕩𝕩 **Start of walk**
- 🛡 **Broch or Fort**
- ✧ **Chambered Cairn**
- ☼ **Mill**
- ▲ **Trig Point**

South Holms

Silva Dale

✧ Ward of Houlland

Skitsack

The Trinks o' Clave

Hagdales Nest

Smoity Loch

Longa Geo

Clave croft ruins

Kidnawater

Loch of Bogligarths

Ness of Collaster

The Kirn of Bauberstong (blow-hole)

Wick of Collaster

Loch of Collaster

▲ Trig Point 216m

Hagmark ✧

Byre of Scord

Spoo Ness

noosts

Longa Water

Black Shun

Lang Holm

Kirkakby

Loch of Quoy

medieval chapel

steep ridge descend with care

South Shun

Brough Holm

WESTING booth

Burn of Righton

Gossa Water

𝕩𝕩 ☼

CIRCULAR WALK C

WESTING BEACH – SILVA DALE
6 miles (10 kms) : 4 hours

OS Maps: Landranger Sheet 1 Shetland – Yell & Unst
Pathfinder Sheet HP 40/50/60 Baltasound

A coastal stroll and then a stiff climb onto the spine of Unst to enjoy the views from Byre of Scord with its nearby trig point, 216m, and an exciting descent back to Westing down the steep side of the hill above Gossawater Loch.

From The Booth at the S end of Westing beach walk round the shingle beach noting Brough Holm which has the remains of a broch on it. Opposite Lang Holm is Kirkaby where there are the barely discernible foundations of a medieval chapel.

The 'Kirn of Bauberstong', a blow hole at the Ayre of Collaster may be seen in action in the right conditions. At Wick of Collaster there are four noosts and extensive croft ruins above the lovely bay where the families living here could also have enjoyed the many attractive geos and waterfalls. The last ruined croft going north in this area is at Clave, and after passing it walk

round Longa Geo and climb up narrow pathway from Hagdales Ness to reach the burn which comes down Silva Dale. Climb east to reach the cairn (158m) on Ward of Houlland and then head south, up past Smoity Loch to reach the 'golf ball' dome covering a navigational aid. The trig point (216m) is just over a wire fence adjacent to the radome on Byre of Scord. One can now use the service road along Valla Field, passing Longa Water on the right before leaving the road when it starts to descend left by walking west to look down over the edge of the ridge. The aim is to now climb down, with care, to go round the south end of Gossa Water and head for Kirk Knowe. Cross the road, which is heading to Newgord where the bridge goes over the Burn of Bighton. On the side of the burn just down from the bridge is a restored water mill, its workings clearly visible. Cross a field to reach The Booth on Westings beach.

Westing.

CIRCULAR WALK D
HOULLAND (LOCH OF CLIFF) – WOODWICK
3 miles (5 kms) : 2 hours

OS Maps: Landranger Sheet 1 Shetland – Yell & Unst
                Pathfinder Sheet HP 51/61 Haroldswick

A short walk down a lovely dale between steep hills to a beach onto which much flotsam and jetsam is deposited by the tide – particularly wood! Geologists can have a field day.

Leave Houlland by taking the track north by climbing over a stout stile. After a few yards take track west by climbing over another stile and follow the track, past a stone sheep shelter, into the hill until it starts to turn south west. Head west across pasture using an old earth bank wall to a fence with a metal gate. Now aim for the valley and by descending the north slopes join the Burn of Dale of Woodwick with the assistance of another stile.

It is an exhilarating experience to come in sight of the sea with the North Holms just offshore and once on the beach explore the ruins of old haaf-fishing booths. The beach can be a mass of wood and plastic but Woodwick can offer other treasure. Quartz, kyanite, mica, felspars and the

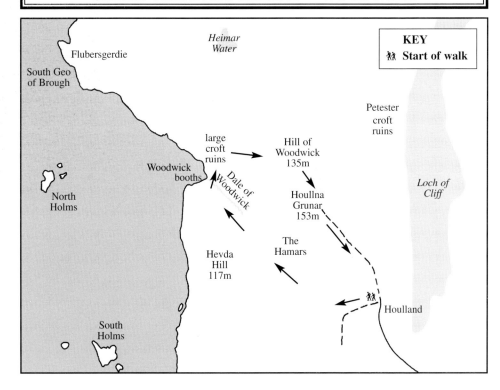

Circular Walk D: HOULLAND – WOODWICK

Heimar Water

Flubersgerdie

South Geo of Brough

KEY
🚶 Start of walk

Petester croft ruins

large croft ruins

Hill of Woodwick 135m

Woodwick booths

Dale of Woodwick

North Holms

Houllna Grunar 153m

Loch of Cliff

Hevda Hill 117m

The Hamars

South Holms

🚶 Houlland

red semi-precious garnets are sometimes discovered on the east coast of Unst, particularly in Woodwick.

One can now return the way one came. Alternatively climb round to the north, not from the beach but slightly inland and view extensive croft ruins overlooking the north end of Woodwick bay. Climb onto Hill of Woodwick (135m) to view deserted crofting area of Petester before aiming south over Voda Mires (123m) to Houllna Gruna (153m). On its south east slope a track descends over Knowe of Boobitten back to Houlland.

Woodwick, looking up the dale from the shore.

Circular Walk E: BURRAFIRTH – HERMA NESS

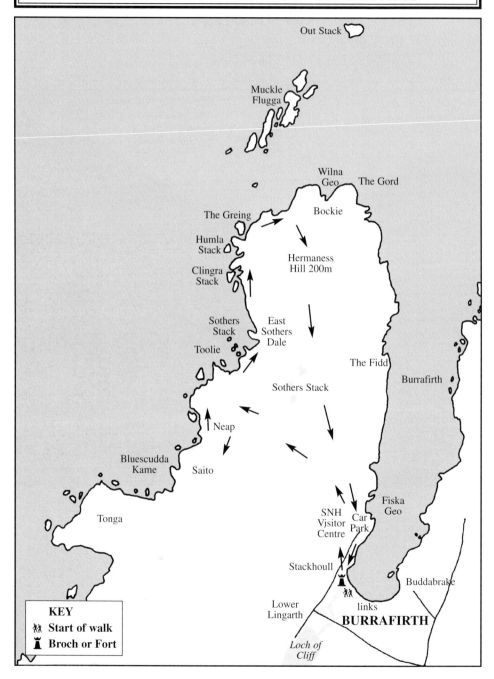

Out Stack

Muckle Flugga

Wilna Geo — The Gord

The Greing — Bockie

Humla Stack

Clingra Stack

Hermaness Hill 200m

Sothers Stack — East Sothers Dale

Toolie

The Fidd

Sothers Stack

Burrafirth

Neap

Bluescudda Kame — Saito

Tonga

Fiska Geo

SNH Visitor Centre — Car Park

Stackhoull

Buddabrake

Lower Lingarth

links

BURRAFIRTH

Loch of Cliff

KEY

🚶 Start of walk

⛫ Broch or Fort

CIRCULAR WALK E

HERMANESS
8 miles (13 kms) : 4 hours

OS Maps: **Landranger Sheet 1 Shetland – Yell & Unst
Pathfinder Sheet HP 51/61 Haroldswick**

A walk which will never be forgotten particularly if it is during the seabird breeding season (puffins breed from mid April to early August). Access to Hermaness National Nature Reserve is unrestricted thanks to courtesy of the owner David Edmonston of Buness whose family began conservation at Hermaness in 1831. The reserve is managed by Scottish Natural Heritage and some routes are way-marked.

The approach to Burrafirth from Haroldswick takes one past the junction left to Quoys. There are often Shetland ponies near the junction who will investigate inside a car if the windows are open. At Quoys until recently was Britain's largest talc quarry and it is worth stopping to look at the deep pit, now filling with water, and pick up a piece of soapstone. A salmon hatchery has been established nearby on the Loch of Cliff.

Gannet colony, Hermaness. Note the chick left foreground.

Hermaness cliff scene.

The Loch of Cliff is protected from the sea by the Links of Burrafirth through which an attractive burn meanders. It is a grazing area which has had occasional use as a football pitch and limited golf course. I played my last game of rugby there, pulling an Achilles tendon enroute to scoring a try and final glory after a rugby career which had spanned 32 years. It included an entry, ten years earlier, in the 1973 Guinness Book of Records concerning a world record rugby defeat 'Roundhay Rams defeated RAF Catterick by 154 points to nil'. I was captain of RAF Catterick but was then posted to Saxa Vord! In the same edition there is a photograph by Bobby Tulloch of the "most tenuously established species of the 474 on the

British Bird list – the male of the sole pair of Snowy Owls found nesting on the Shetland Island of Fetlar."

A ruined mill can be seen near the northern shore of the loch and one ascends to Hermaness with the croft house of Stackhoull on the left hand side of the road. Shortly after this, on the right hand side of the road and below it, is the broch of Burra Firth. Cross the field down to a stile over a wire fence and onto a small rocky headland. Under 60ft in diameter the broch is hidden beneath a grassy mound but many stones project through the turf. It is a broch easily overlooked because in summer it is a place where undergrowth survives to disguise what is underneath. The mound was protected by one and possibly by two earthen ramparts on the landward side. Further along the narrow road the former Muckle Flugga Lighthouse Shore Station comes into view but follow the road left which brings one out into the car-park for Herma Ness National Nature Reserve.

There is a large notice board giving information and a map of the reserve. The reserve also has a warden, from whom advice can be sought during the summer, based at the Scottish Natural Heritage visitor centre in a flat at the shore station. Go through the stiles and ascend the footpath on to the reserve. At Burn of Winnaswarta continue along the way-marked path heading west using helpful duck boards in marshy areas. On reaching the cliffs head south to Bluescudda Kame and Saito which have large seabird colonies of fulmar, puffin, gannet, kittiwakes, guillemot and razorbill. Watch out for great skuas (bonxies) and Arctic skuas (aalins) as you cross their nesting grounds.

Return to the way-marked path but now head north along the cliffs. The peninsula is approximately 3 miles by 1 mile and the cliffs rise from 200 – 500ft. It is magnificent walking north and looking down from Neap and Toolie on the many stacks and skerries. Puffins can be found at various places along the top of the cliffs here. Descend to East Sothers Dale, a perfect spot for a picnic lunch and ascend to climb round the lower reaches of Herma Ness Hill, past many more stacks, to where a track

Bluescudda Kame, Hermaness.

joins the coastline at Boelie. This part of the peninsula is as close to Muckle Flugga that one can get. Above there used to be a signal hut to which a lighthouse keeper on shore duty used to come daily from Burrafirth Shore Station to look across to the lighthouse and send or receive signals. In 1939 a radio transmitter/receiver was installed. The lighthouse was built in 1854, designed by Thomas Stevenson, father of Robert Louis Stevenson. Robert illustrated his book 'Treasure Island' with a map which is similar to the outline map of Unst. The lighthouse cost £32,378 15s. 5d to build and on the north opposes an almost precipitous front to the surging seas. The sea on one occasion broke open a door of the lighthouse 185ft above sea level!

The lighthouse appears to be closer to the shore than it really is and is now unmanned.

At The Gord there is a 14 inch metal post from where we can look a short distance north to the Out Stack, the furthest north point of Her Majesty's British Dominions. It is difficult to imagine anybody going out there but there are records of fishermen clinging to the tang attached to this rock for six hours awaiting

Warden's hut, Hermaness, taken in the 1920s.

After the gale of 1991. Flowers placed on the site of the warden's hut.

rescue and many a sailing ship was wrecked there before the lighthouse was built.

The most famous visitor to date was Lady Jane Franklin, wife of Sir John, the Arctic explorer, who disappeared whilst leading an expedition to seek the North West Passage in 1845. Jessie Saxby, daughter of Dr. L. Edmonstone, described Lady Franklin's visit to Unst in 1849.

"When Lady Franklin was wandering over Britain in eager quest for men to go and search for Sir John and his companions she came to Unst and asked to be taken to the most northerly spot where she could look over the sea and – as she said – 'send love on the wings of prayer', to the ill fated adventurer. The weather chanced to be exceptionally fine and my father, with a picked crew and a famous boat, took Lady Franklin to set foot, where never woman's foot has been, on the grim and lonesome Ootstaa (Out Stack) …

Those who were with her said she stood for some minutes on the sombre rock, quite silent, tears falling slowly, and her hands stretched out towards the north … She returned with some sea weed as a souvenir. Ten years later she learned that Sir John had perished in the ice in 1847.

In the summer there is intense sea bird activity on the various colonies both onshore and offshore and after turning to admire the view east from The Framd the return route to Burra Firth should be planned. The eastern coast of Herma Ness is quite varied above Burra Firth and there are many geos, so unless you are still feeling particularly energetic it is recommended that return is made on the well defined track. It connects with the Scottish Natural Heritage way-marked route on Hermaness Hill, on the southern slope of which once stood the warden's hut. The hut was destroyed and the lives of two young walkers lost on New Years Eve 1991 in a terrible gale.

78

CIRCULAR WALK F

SKAW
6 miles (10 kms) : 3-4 hours

OS Maps: Landranger Sheet 1 Shetland – Yell & Unst
                  Pathfinder Sheet HP 51/61 Haroldswick

A new road now takes one from Norwick and over the hill, via the Devil's Elbow to link with the old road to Skaw. Enjoy a walk round Britain's most northerly house and beach to view the impressive cliffs on the NE slopes of Saxa Vord.

At Skaw note a salmon hatchery, house (The Haa) and an upturned lifeboat, from the collier *Sea Venture* torpedoed in 1939, which saved all the crew. Cross the footbridge to the lovely sandy beach and note in the heavily eroded cliffs the remains of prehistoric houses excavated in 1972 but which will probably disappear for all time shortly. Pass the remains of four noosts and then a stile helps one on the way round Skaw. The headland is littered with World War 2 ruined buildings including retired toilets looking rather forlorn. Note the cave and beacon on Holm of Skaw before walking round the large geos at Forn and Gorsun. A stone built sheep shelter wall on Hill Ness, which has a good view of Muckle Flugga seen through the gap between The Noup and The Lug, is the only form of shelter after Skaw. Round the bay at Brei Wick look down on the Noup where an iron-age promontory fort site has been identified. Haul yourself up the slopes of Saxa

The Haa, Skaw.

79

Muckle Flugga viewed between The Noup and The Lug. Outstack on the right. Note 'Da Claw o' da Lug'.

Circular Walk F: SKAW – THE NOUP

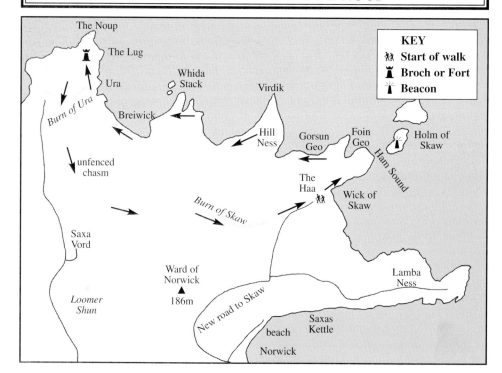

KEY
🚶 Start of walk
♜ Broch or Fort
☼ Beacon

The Noup

The Lug

Ura

Whida
Stack

Virdik

Burn of Ura

Breiwick

Hill
Ness

Gorsun
Geo

Foin
Geo

Holm of
Skaw

unfenced
chasm

The
Haa

Wick of
Skaw

Ham Sound

Burn of Skaw

Saxa
Vord

Ward of
Norwick

Lamba
Ness

Loomer
Shun

186m

New road to Skaw

beach

Saxas
Kettle

Norwick

Vord toward the military installation fence by crossing the Burn of Ura where James Hay once panned for gold. On a plateau high above Breiwick beware an evil chasm in an area marked by four metal posts but no wire. A legend puts the giant Saxa in a cleft hereabouts and he is very welcome to it. Keep to the high ground until you link up with the Burn of Skaw which can be followed all the way back down to The Haa.

Lifeboat of *Sea Venture* now a shed roof at Britain's most northerly house.

CIRCULAR WALK G

LAMBA NESS
3 miles (5 kms) : 2 hours

OS Maps: Landranger Sheet 1 Shetland – Yell & Unst
            Pathfinder Sheet HP 51/61 Haroldswick

A stroll out to a peninsula where the sea can rage and birds seek sanctuary in stormy weather. Saxa's kettle may not be boiling but in season mushrooms abound.

In order to start the walk take the new road to

Skaw from Norwick and leave it at a cattle grid where the old military road heads east. One can stick to the road all the way out to Lamba Ness, passing the ruins of the World War 2 signals unit RAF Skaw. However it is worth walking the southern cliffs to view Saxa's kettle. This is

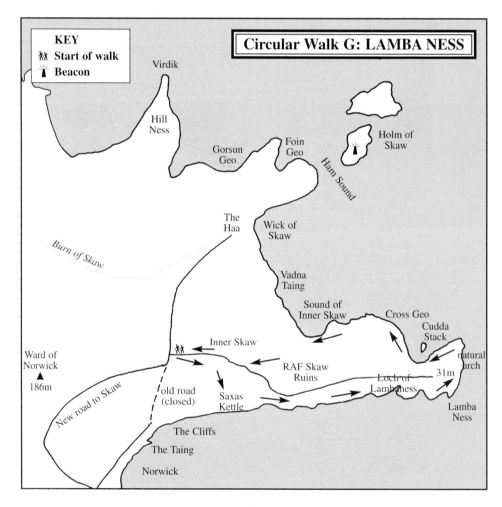

an unusual stack, close to the cliff side which has a tunnel at its base through which the sea flows into a circular rock basin. Here the giant Saxa Vord used to prepare his food and when his rival Herman asked to use it in order to prepare a Whale casserole he demanded a half of the Whale as a fee. This so incensed Herman that he threw a rock at Saxa (Herman's Stack) and in response Saxa threw a similar sized boulder (Saxa'a Baa). The ground gradually rises to the point of Lamba Ness past a loch and masts down from which is a natural arch.

Walk the northern banks to Sand of Inner Skaw before returning to the 'military' road on Inner Skaw and so back to the start point.

Saxa's Kettle, Lamba Ness.

CIRCULAR WALK H

THE HEOGS, NIKKA VORD AND CRUSSA FIELD
4 miles (6½ kms) : 2 hours

OS Maps: Landranger Sheet 1 Shetland – Yell & Unst
Pathfinder Sheet HP 51/61 Haroldswick

A heritage walk with splendid views exploring mainly prehistoric cairns on the hills between Baltasound and Haroldswick. This was also an important quarrying area for iron chromate.

On the road north from Baltasound, just north of Hagdale on the climb up towards Setters Hill Quarry, a ladder stile will be seen on the left which crosses the stone wall. Climb over the wall and walk up to Little Heog (124m) where a much dilapidated cairn will be seen. Its debris was estimated to cover a circular area of about 45ft 9ins in diameter.

Walk across to Muckle Heog, 40m; on the summit of this hill are the remains of a large heel-shaped cairn built of rough irregular blocks of weathered serpentine gathered from the hillside. No sign of either a chamber or cist can

now be seen but during the 1860s, when a fishing signal station was being erected at the site of the cairn, two cists were unearthed. One contained a larger number of human skulls and bones whilst the other contained a skull, ox bones and six urns. 100ft lower down the western summit is a gully and adjacent to a field wall a better preserved cairn, Muckle Heog West, can be seen. Originally it was thought to contain four cists, two of which are still visible and Hibbert records that in 1760 two bodies were found near the base of the cairn. Probably dating back to the Bronze Age this cairn is the only definite example known of the combination of a heel-shaped cairn with cists rather than a central chamber.

Return to the peak of Muckle Heog and descend on the northern slope about 250 yards to the

Muckle Heog East heel shaped cairn.

84

cairn known as 'Harold's Grave'. Traditionally, Haroldswick is considered the landing place of Harald Harfagri in 872AD after he had touched at Funzie, Fetlar and then made for Unst to begin subduing the Shetland Vikings. The 'Harold's Grave' shown on Muckle Heog cannot be his as he is buried near Haugesund, Norway. Today the cairn is just a heap of loose stones 50ft x 25ft. Hibbert records that the cairn had been opened some years before 1822 and certainly nothing was found in 1865. Two beautiful bronze ornaments are reported to have been found in this cairn at some time which, with its shape, strengthens the theory that the cairn is of a Viking origin.

Now proceed west over Nikka Vord across The Dale and up to the peak of Crussa Field (143m) the highest part of the ridge that overlooks the upper part of Baltasound. On this ridge are two groups of ancient monuments.

1. Three scattered cairns on the summit, the largest of which was a burial cairn as it contains a central cist amidst its 40ft diameter. The cist measured nearly 4ft long, 3ft broad and 2ft deep. Nothing is known of what it once contained.

2. Rounds of Tivla. 200 yards downhill to the SE of the summit are the remains of three

Circular Walk H: THE HEOGS – CRUSSA FIELD

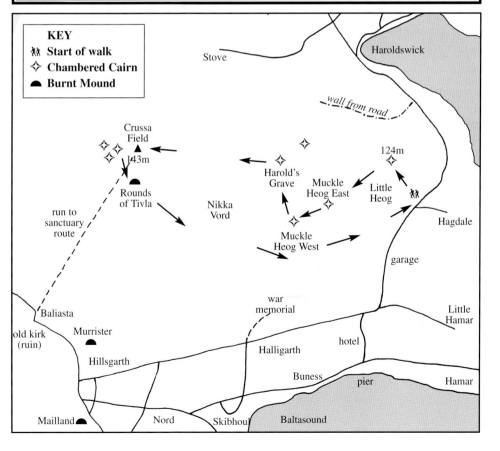

KEY
- 𝌆 **Start of walk**
- ✧ **Chambered Cairn**
- ▲ **Burnt Mound**

circular earthworks. One retains its recorded form consisting of three low concentric banks with two shallow ditches between surrounding a central stony mound spread some 13ft in diameter. The remains of two other earthworks lie respectively 28ft and 48ft to the E and SW of the main round.

From this vantage point looking down SW to Baliasta and SE to Baltasound it is easy to believe the local legends concerning Crussa Field. Of the holding of the Norse 'Althing' for the islands here before finally being transferred to Tingwall. Of criminals sentenced to death being allowed a dash down its stony slopes through the assembled people in the hope of, in pre-Christian times, making the sanctuary of a stone circle at Baliasta or in Christian times to the Kirk of Baliasta. Where those who were stoned to death on their descent were buried crosses were cut into the turf and from these crosses the hill derives its name.

Return to the start point by heading back east the way you came or follow the fleeing fugitives route (by running?) down to Baliasta and returning to Hagdale by road, a distance from ruined Baliasta Kirk of 3 miles (5 kms).

Kirk of Baliasta.

CIRCULAR WALK I
THE KEEN OF HAMAR NATIONAL NATURE RESERVE
2 miles (3 kms) : 2 hours

OS Maps: **Landranger Sheet 1 Shetland – Yell & Unst**
Pathfinder Sheet HP 40/50/60 Baltasound
HP 51/61 Haroldswick

Nestling in the stony ground of the Keen of Hamar are some of the rarest plants in Britain. This walk takes one onto The National Nature Reserve (Scottish Natural Heritage leaflet available: Tel 01595 693345) and includes the disused mineral workings and Horse Mill at Hagdale.

North of Baltasound where the main road takes a significant bend near a bus shelter a minor road heads east to Littlehamar. Scottish Natural Heritage has provided an information board from which access to the Reserve is by a gate. The Keen of Hamar once had an active coastguard lookout at its peak (89m) and the

Shetland's only unique plant. Edmondston's Chickweed (*Cerastium nigrescens*). Discovered by local botanist Thomas Edmondston of Buness in 1837. The large white flowers can be seen from June to August.

area can look quite desolate made up as it is by serpentine rock which has weathered to form an area of stones. This landscape, described as 'lunar', looks today how much of Britain looked at the end of the Ice Age. At the right time of the year the vegetation is rich in flowers, grasses and sedges. Of particular note are Norwegian sandwort, early purple orchid (flowers late May and June) and rarest of all, Edmonston's chickweed, discovered in 1837 by Thomas Edmonston of Buness.

Descend west on the north side of the reserve to cross a cattle corridor and reach a larger ladder stile which gives access to the disused mineral quarries area. Walk through the workings towards the main road and a building (the Masonic Lodge for Unst) visiting the partially restored Horse Mill. In this circular mill horses, treading the paved way inside it, turned the mill stones to grind the iron chromate. The chromate remained in the central reservoir until the impurities were flushed away by water which runs into the stone socket onto the revolving stones.

Walk the main road back to the junction to Little Hamar where one can turn east back to the start point.

Circular Walk I: THE KEEN OF HAMAR

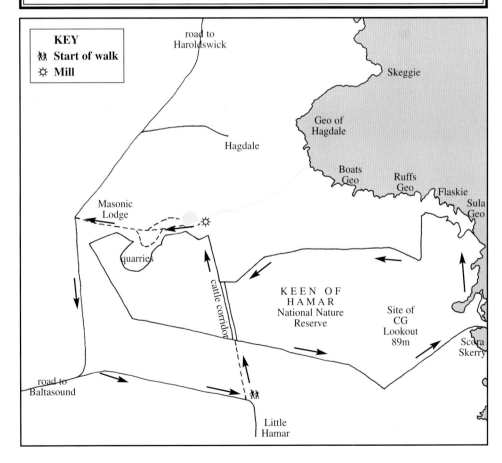

KEY
🚶 Start of walk
☼ Mill

road to Haroldswick

Skeggie

Geo of Hagdale

Hagdale

Boats Geo

Ruffs Geo

Flaskie

Sula Geo

Masonic Lodge

quarries

cattle corridor

KEEN OF HAMAR
National Nature Reserve

Site of CG Lookout 89m

Scora Skerry

road to Baltasound

Little Hamar

Fragrant orchid, Keen of Hamar.

Cerastium arctium, **Keen of Hamar.**

Horse Mill, Hagdale. Clibberswick, in background

CIRCULAR WALK J ▮

SANDWICK AND MUNESS CASTLE

5 miles (8 kms) : 3 hours

OS Maps: Landranger Sheet 1 Shetland – Yell & Unst
Pathfinder Sheet HP 40/50/60 Baltasound

NorNova Knitwear, Muness, which displays local craft and knitwear, lies on this route and offers tea and snacks. Walking is easy going and the walk can easily be extended north to include Colvadale.

A heritage walk of enormous variety including as it does, a lovely beach with a Pictish grave

site, a medieval Norse longhouse ruin, a medieval chapel and notable Muness Castle.

Muness Castle is the start point for this walk. The key is available from the white croft opposite. Built in 1598 the castle is well worth exploring; note the round towers and hanging turrets, the "gun holes" and inscription on a

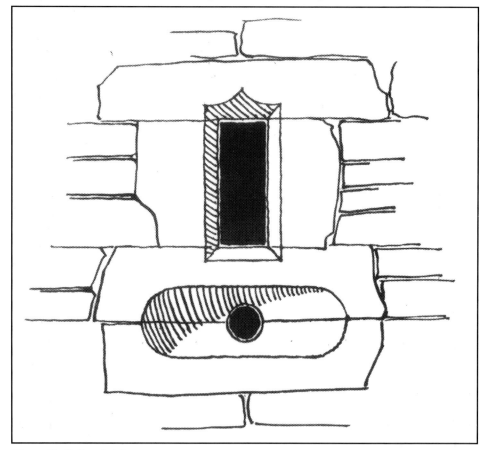

Muness Castle "gun hole".

90

panel above the doorway in the south wall. It was only inhabited for a hundred years being unoccupied after 1699 when the last direct heir, Andrew Bruce, was drowned.

Walk the road heading west until a cattle grid after which a former track is discernible which heads up north to the delightfully restored croft house of Hannigarth (self-catering). Note a

Circular Walk J: MUNESS CASTLE – SANDWICK

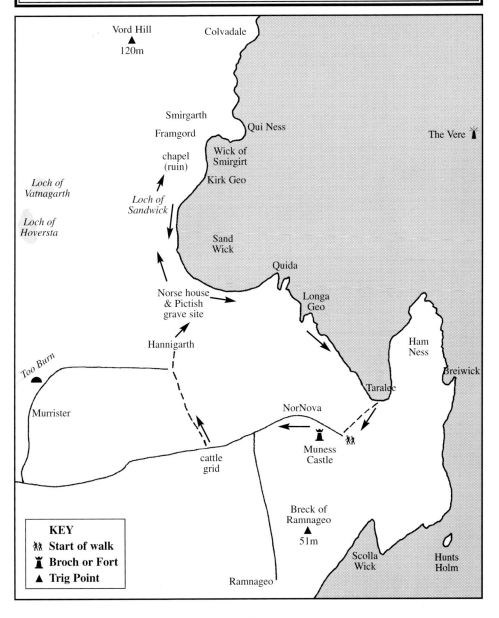

Vord Hill
▲
120m

Colvadale

Smirgarth

Framgord

Qui Ness

The Vere 🔥

chapel
(ruin)

Wick of
Smirgirt

Loch of
Vatnagarth

Kirk Geo

Loch of
Sandwick

Loch of
Hoversta

Sand
Wick

Quida

Norse house
& Pictish
grave site

Longa
Geo

Ham
Ness

Hannigarth

Breiwick

Too Burn

Taralee

Murrister

NorNova

Muness
Castle

cattle
grid

Breck of
Ramnageo
▲
51m

KEY
👥 Start of walk
🏰 Broch or Fort
▲ Trig Point

Scolla
Wick

Hunts
Holm

Ramnageo

World War 2 mine and cross over a stile to walk down to the white sandy beach of Sandwick where Shetland's sole dated Pictish burial was excavated. A single skeleton was found below a low rectangular cairn made of quartz pebbles and edged with upright stone slabs. On the beach also are the ruins of a Norse – medieval period house dating from the late thirteenth or early fourteenth century.

Above Kirk Geo at Framgord is the ancient ruined St. Mary's Chapel within a burial ground. This is particularly interesting as it contains ancient upright stones with crosses and recumbent stones with a cross or a central rib on the upper surfaces. In the NW corner are buried three of the crew of the Norwegian ship *Hop* from Bergen who gave their lives when the ship was torpedoed on 4th February, 1940. Other members of the crew are buried at Baliasta, Fetlar and Lunna. Other dangers still lurk

offshore, particularly the rocks known as The Vere due east offshore from Sandwick. Mariners are warned of its danger when they see the red light shine from the lighthouse at the south end of Balta Island. In 1939 a Greek ship *Torre Chandros* carrying iron-ore hit The Vere but happily all the crew were saved.

Retrace your steps back to the beach at Sandwick and keeping to the shore line pass a small ruin, cross a stile and burn to reach a ruined booth by a stone enclosure. A solitary planticrub survives. A number of small geos indent the coastline of which Longa Geo is the deepest.

At the shingle beach at the head of the small bay, Ham of Muness, is Taralee where a road goes up from the shore bringing one back to Muness Castle and refreshments at NorNova.

George Jamieson and David Waters at the German's Grave, Colvadale.

CIRCULAR WALK K ████████████████

BELMONT – UYEASOUND
5 miles (8 kms) : 3 hours

OS Maps: Landranger Sheet 1 Shetland – Yell & Unst
Pathfinder Sheet HP 40/50/60 Baltasound
HP 59/69 Fetlar north

A fine introductory walk to Unst which includes a gentle stroll along the coast, a walk round delightful Uyeasound and a climb over Gallow Hill with its impressive views.

From the ferry terminal at Belmont head south along the banks to Head of Mulla noting the salmon cages. Salmon farming plays an important part in the Shetland economy and villages such as Uyeasound have benefited from it. At Head of Mulla in the middle of the land of

the abandoned croft is a late iron age oval house site which has produced pottery of the wheel house type.

Go round the Loch of Heogland to reach the Holm of Heogland which has a cairn; access to this small tidal island is possible at low water. From Point of Burkwell one has a complete view of Uyea island as one enters the Sound; keep a look out for the grave of a drowned sailor marked by long flat stones at head and

Circular Walk K: BELMONT – UYEASOUND

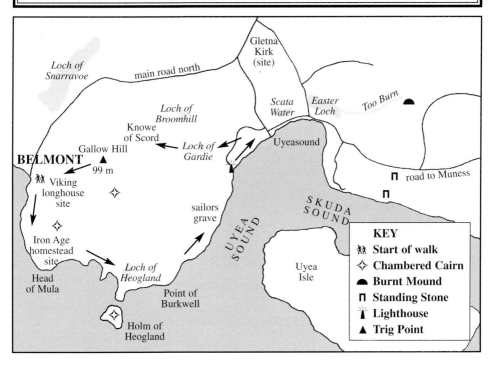

foot and always with a garland of sea shells on top. There are ancient noosts and an old pier – a reminder of the days when Uyeasound was a busy herring fishing station. Pass the lighthouse and arrive at the Uyeasound Pier and the Westside shop near which are public toilets and the Gardiesfauld Hostel. At anytime of the year it is worth visiting Scata Water and Easter Loch both of which attract a variety of duck and, in winter, whooper swans.

To return to Belmont from Gardie ascend the Knowe of Scord with the Lochs of Gardie and Broomhill on your right. Keep some time in hand to explore the summit of Gallow Hill which at the trig point is 300ft (99m) high. Within an enclosure adjoining two sheep shelters is a much-dilapidated cairn. Gallow Hill has been used during war time as a look-out station and stones from another cairn just south of the trig point were used to construct a shelter, so practically no trace of the original cairn remains. In 1825 stone cists had been found under it with the remains of a human skeleton and some limpet shells. On the south shoulder at 200ft are the dilapidated remains of a cairn which originally had a diameter of 30ft.

Gallow Hill is a magnificent viewing point from which descend back to the ferry terminal at Belmont by crossing two stone walls and following a track which runs down the NW to the main road just north of the pier head. You will pass beneath a partially excavated early Viking longhouse on a bluff of land above the ferry terminal car park.

An otter spotted at Westing.

CIRCULAR WALK L

UYEA ISLE
5 miles (8 kms) : 3 hours

OS Maps: **Landranger Sheet 1 Shetland – Yell & Unst**
                Pathfinder Sheet HP 59/69 Fetlar north

The uninhabited island of Uyea is a lovely island to explore and for its size contains many interesting features including prehistoric burial sites. There is a medieval chapel and the impressive ruins of Uyea Hall, once the home of the last Conservative MP to represent Orkney and Shetland at the House of Commons.

First visit the hall which although now in a derelict state has ruins which are most imposing and can be see from afar. A similar house to it, which is still very much lived in, will be found at Brough House near the old pier in Burravoe, Yell.

It was once the home of Major Basil Neven-Spence, MP for Orkney and Shetland (1935-1950) and graves of the Neven-Spence family will be seen in the burial ground at the Chapel which lies to the SE of the hall. The chapel, though ruined, originally consisted of a nave and chancel both dating back to the 12th century. The walls are built of the local schist and lime mortar and are still almost complete. Inside are the remains of a table-tombstone, in two halves. Both halves have decoration and the memorial is thought to commemorate John Ross, a merchant of Uyeasound in the 17th century.

Uyea Hall.

In the burial ground ancient small crosses and upright slabs are to be seen SE of the chapel.

From the chapel walk NE to Tur Ness where there are the remains of an ancient settlement in three areas containing remains of circular constructions, ditches, mounds and banks. From here follow the coastline round Brei Wick and Hawks Ness to Winna Ness. Here on a knoll in about 1860 a grave, set round with eight oblong stones on end in a circle, was opened but only revealed a thighbone!

Complete the walk round the coastline to arrive back at the landing place at Cliva Skerries. About 70 yards west in the north shore about

Circular Walk L: UYEA ISLE

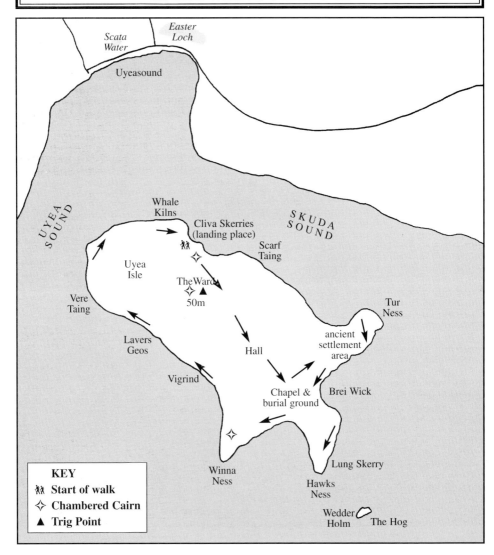

Scata Water

Easter Loch

Uyeasound

UYEA SOUND

Whale Kilns

Cliva Skerries (landing place)

SKUDA SOUND

Scarf Taing

Uyea Isle

The Ward

Vere Taing

50m

Tur Ness

Lavers Geos

Hall

ancient settlement area

Vigrind

Chapel & burial ground

Brei Wick

Lung Skerry

Winna Ness

Hawks Ness

KEY
弃 Start of walk
✧ Chambered Cairn
▲ Trig Point

Wedder Holm

The Hog

96

Uyea Isle Chapel and ancient memorials.

Cairn on Winna Ness, Uyea Isle.

50ft above the sea is a chambered cairn. Both the passage and chamber are much destroyed. On the top of The Ward are the remains of two cairns, both dilapidated. A number of urns were recovered from them, each containing burnt bones and three urns, of the Bronze Age type, which are now in the National Museum with a fragment of a sculptured stone urn cover.

John Brand reported in 1701 that:
"In Uzia an Isle lying nigh to Unst, there is a Mettal gotten having the colour of Gold, which several of the Dutch Merchants have taken with them to Hamburgh, and tried it there, but by the force of time it did not become Liquid, but crumbled into small pieces; It is to be had there in great plenty. This sheweth there may be minerals in these Isles tho not known nor searched for."

In July 1680 three Uyea girls rowed over to milk some cows on Haaf Gruney but on their way back were caught in a severe westerly gale. Eventually they ended up safely on the coast of Norway where they were made so welcome they all married, settled down and lived happily ever after!

Shetland sixareen, by John Tudor's illustrator 'CWHH'.

CIRCULAR WALK M

BALTA ISLAND
4 miles (6 kms) : 2 hours

OS Maps: **Landranger Sheet 1 Shetland – Yell & Unst**
                    Pathfinder Sheet HP 40/50/60 Baltasound

A sandy island, a delightful place to explore with views looking back to Baltasound or out to the open sea.

Rabbits abound on this island probably because nobody has lived permanently here for centuries. There was a medieval chapel dedicated to St. Sunniva on Balta but the site has yet to be found. Jessie Saxby reported that in about 1900 men building a fishing station close to the shore dug up a quantity of human bones. Was this the burial ground of St. Sunniva's Chapel? It was thought not because the bodies had been flung together anyhow in a mass grave. Were they then the bones of Picts and Norse Warriors who had fought, so tradition said, a battle of Balta? Jessie Saxby however recalled the story of a ship putting into Balta Sound with plague-stricken men on board. She thought it likely that the bones were those of plague victims who were buried on Balta by their shipmates.

The sandy beach of North Links is perfect for a picnic which can be walked off by a stroll round Pussi Geos to the lighthouse at the south end.

Geo of the Brough, Balta Isle.

Circular Walk M: BALTA ISLE

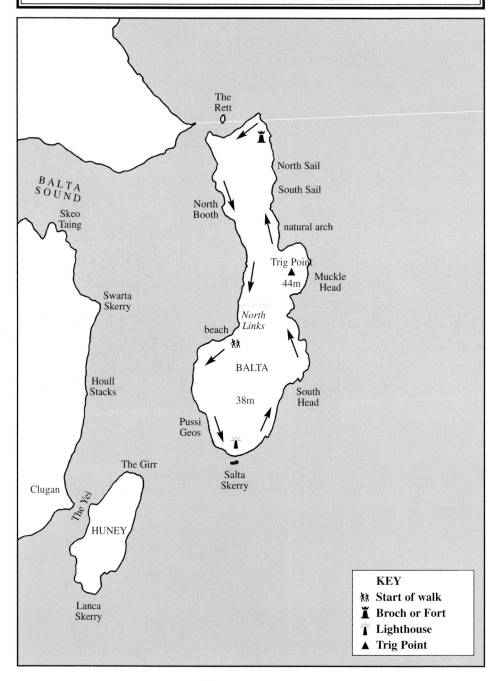

The
Rett

North Sail

South Sail

BALTA
SOUND

Skeo
Taing

North
Booth

natural arch

Trig Point
▲
44m

Muckle
Head

Swarta
Skerry

*North
Links*

beach

BALTA

Houll
Stacks

38m

South
Head

Pussi
Geos

The Girr

Clugan

Salta
Skerry

The Yei

HUNEY

Lanca
Skerry

KEY

🚶 **Start of walk**

♜ **Broch or Fort**

🗼 **Lighthouse**

▲ **Trig Point**

Walk north past Southhead to climb to the trig point at Mucklehead (44m). In the north-east end of the island there is a ruin of a broch built on a stack, the lower part of which is joined to the mainland. Access is difficult and is not recommended. Return to North Links passing the narrows of the Rett, noting remains of herring industry piers, for Balta island was an extension of Baltasound when the herring industry was at its peak.

Trig point above Muckle Head, Balta Isle. The cliffs of Hamar in the background.

1. GEOLOGY

The geological map of Unst gives vivid illustrations of the complicated geological history of the island. Glaciation had an important effect in Unst for the land ice from Scandinavia found in Unst its first obstacle. It simply rode straight over the island and was partly responsible for the evacuation of the central valley.

Round the island one finds:
Westing – striped horneblendic and calc-sillcate rocks and gneisses
Burrafirth – garnet-tourmaline, siliceous and felspathic gneisses
Vallafield – garnet-staurolite kyanite gneisses
Saxa Vord – augen granite
Norwick – group of graphitic and horneblendic schists
Muness – phyllites and conglomerates

as well as areas of:
Limestone, greenstone, pyroxene and serpentine.
Chromite/serpentine – first quarry 1824.
Platinum and kyanite both assessed for commercial exploitation.
Talc development came during the 20th century
Asbestos is present in various small veins,
Gold in Saxa Vord?

2. BIRDS AND MAMMALS

As noted by Gifford in 1733 Unst has, "plenty of little horses", and was, until recently, one of the two places in Shetland that had a pony sale each year.

Otters may be spotted along the shore, most likely along the east coast between Belmont and Uyeasound. They eat mainly fish such as butterfish and eels but will also take breeding duck and black guillemots.

Shetland sheep, renowned for their fine soft wool, will be seen in plenty providing the raw material for the home knitting industry. Unst has been particularly famous for the fine lace shawls some of its highly skilled ladies have been able to produce. Sheep increased in the island as the number of cattle decreased.

Birds, however, are what most visitors come to see and Unst has three major wintering sites of wild fowl (whooper swans, tufted, pochard, mallard, wigeon, golden-eye ducks) on the Loch of Cliff, Loch of Snarra Voe and Easter and Wester Lochs. In some years over 100 whooper swans have been counted on Easter Loch.

Along the coast fulmars will be found all the year round and in the summer 25% of the total British puffin population is here, 30% of black guillemots, 25% Arctic terns and 30% of the shags. The proportion is even higher for the skuas: 90% of great skuas and 70% Arctic skuas. Gannets, kittiwakes, razorbills and guillemots will also be found in plenty.

TAKING THE BOOTS OFF ...

This completes this walking guide to Unst. In the words of the hymn on page 48 hopefully you have not had to "wander from the pathway" too much. We found King Lear somewhere along the way and if the walk has gone well the magic of Shetland will have worked its spell and you will have fallen in love with Unst. It now would be appropriate to return to Shakespeare and his sonnet 27. For as you stagger off the coastal path, the "Round Unst Trek" completed, it could be a case of:

"Weary with toil, I haste me to my bed,
The dear repose for limbs with travel tired."

and later, home once more, recapture the walk in your imagination – and make plans to return to Britain's most northerly isle again one day!

"But then begins a journey in my head
To work my mind when body's work's expired;
For then my thoughts, from far where I abide,
Intend a jealous pilgrimage to thee ..."

A box-bed

ACKNOWLEDGEMENTS

I am indebted to the authors of the following books and magazine articles:

Unst: My Island Home and it's Story.	Charles Sandison	1968
Unst	Unst Council of Social Service	
Shetland Traditional Lore	Jessie Saxby	1932
Shetland Folk Lore	John Spence	1899
Places Names of Shetland	Jakob Jakobsen	1936
Shetland Dictionary	John Graham	1979
Natural History of Shetland	R. J. Berry & J. L. Johnson	1980
The Medieval Churches and Chapels of Shetland	R. G. Cant	1975
A Guide to Prehistoric Shetland	Noel Fojut	1981
A Guide to Shetland Mammals	Bobby Tulloch	1978
Letters on Shetland	Peter Jamieson	1949
A Description of the Shetland Islands	Samuel Hibbert	1822
Shetland	Robert Cowie	1874
Guide to Shetland	T. M. Y. Manson	1942
The Orkneys and Shetland	John R. Tudor	1883
Pictures from Shetlands Past	Fred Irvine	1955
Shetland III ("The Inventory")		
The Ancient and Historic Monuments of Scotland	Royal Commission	1946
Reminiscences of a Voyage to Shetland	Christian Ployen	1896
A Brief Description of Orkney, Zetland etc	John Brand	1701
Description of Zetland Islands	Thomas Gifford	1733
The Island of Unst	R. T. Wheeler and members of	
	The Geographical Field Group	
	Nottingham University	1964
Scottish Diver Magazine 'E49'	Andy Carter	
The Pennine Way	Christopher John Wright	1967
Shetland Life Magazine	Ed. J. R. Nicolson	
Churches in Unst	Elisabeth Nicolson	
Arthur Robertson – 'E49'		
Sam Polson – Unst articles		
Orkney and Shetland	George Low	1774
Art Rambles in Shetland	John Reid	1869
Songs and Sights of Shetland	Christine M. Guy	1995
A Guide to Shetland's Breeding Birds	Bobby Tulloch	1992
The Chambered tombs of Scotland Vol 1 & 2	Audrey Shore Henshall	1965
Burnt Mound papers (including extracts from		
National Monuments record of Scotland up to 1989)	John Cruse	
Noost	Frank Renwick	1978
Iron Age Promontory Forts in the Northern Isles	Raymond Lamb	
BAR Series 79		
Shetland – an illustrated architectural guide	Mike Finnie	1990
Coastal Settlements of the North,		
Scottish Archaeological Forum Vol 5	Raymond Lamb	1973
Bobby Tulloch's Shetland	Bobby Tulloch	1988

Thanks to all those past and present who helped me to know and appreciate Unst, in one way or another. Of particular help with this book were my late wife Christine, John Cluness, Pam Mouat, Barbara Priest, Harry Edwards, Sam Polson, Magnie Sinclair, Wg Cdr Ron Sparkes, George Jamieson, Mrs W. Jamieson, Willie Laurenson, Andrew Laurenson, Minnie Mouatt, Mary Sutherland, Duncan and Janet Sandison, David and Jennifer Edmonston, Norman Moir, Mary Ouroussoff and Catherine Ginger.

Mary Helen Odie and the Trustees of the Old Haa Trust, Burravoe, Yell, for access to and the use of the following photographs by Bobby Tulloch: *Cerastium Edmonstonii*, Sea Rocket, Fragrant Orchid, *Cerastium Arctium*, Herma Ness, Muckle Flugga, Skaw, Norwick, bonxie, puffins, gannets, otter and Westing.

Liam O'Neill copyright paintings of Haroldswick and Norwick. Muckle Flugga: Charles Tait. The Shetland Islands Council inter-island ferry crews.

Unst Heritage Trust for the use of the photographs of the 'Grace Darling', Warden's Hut, Herma Ness and Herring Boats, Baltasound.

The Royal Commission on the Ancient and Historical Monuments of Scotland for the photographs of Hoga Ness Broch plan, Gun Hole Muness Castle drawing, Balta Geo of Broch and Muckle Heog East Cairn.

Box bed illustration – John Reid
Scottish Natural Heritage for maps of Herma Ness and Keen of Hamar.
Ronnie Gallagher – Submarine E49 photograph.
Shetland Museum – Curator – Tommy Watt, for the photograph of Springfield Station, Baltasound 1906.
Methodist Conference – The hymn tune 'Norwick'.
Christine Guy – photographs of author at Goturm's Hole; Solstice swim at Skaw; and Easter Loch, Uyeasound.

Map of Unst by Ann R. Thomas.
All other photographs are copyright of the Author.

All publications in this series owe their existence to the 'Around the Isles' articles by "Hundiclock" published in 'Sullom Voe Scene'. Grateful thanks to Janet Mullins who once again has worked hard and given of her time to prepare this book for publication.

Details of accommodation available in Unst are published each year by Shetland Islands Tourism, Lerwick. Telephone (01959) 693434.

Muckle Flugga and puffins.